MUSTANG

THE OPERATIONAL RECORD

Robert Jackson

Smithsonian Institution Press
Washington, D.C.

This edition first published in the United States of America
in 1993 by Smithsonian Institution Press.

First published in the United Kingdom in 1992 by
Airlife Publishing Ltd.

Library of Congress Catalog Card Number 92-85555

ISBN 1-56098-253-5

Manufactured in England.

Contents

Acknowledgements

I HAVE received help from many quarters in the preparation of this book, but I would like to make special mention of the Air Historical Branch, MoD (RAF) for providing information on RAF Mustang tactical recce operations; to Air Marshal Sir Frederick Sowrey and Mr Harry Holmes for much assistance with photographic material; and to Ann Tilbury for her diligent photographic research.

Introduction

THIS IS THE operational history of the North American P-51 Mustang, one of the most remarkable combat aircraft of all time.

It is not a story of Mustang 'aces', nor of the achievements of individual units that flew the aircraft operationally. It is, rather, the story of an aircraft which, evolved to meet a specific operational requirement, eventually went far beyond the expectations of that requirement and exercised a profound influence on the outcome of the air war in all theatres between 1942 and 1945.

The story of the Mustang does not end there. Long after the Second World War was over, the Mustang had a key part to play in other, more limited conflicts such as the Korean War and the Sinai campaign of 1956. Indeed, without the swift intervention of USAF Mustang units, the war in Korea might well have been lost in its opening weeks, with disastrous consequences for the stability of the Far East.

This book is intended as a tribute to those who designed this amazing and versatile aircraft, and to the thousands who flew it in combat.

Robert Jackson

Chapter 1
Concept of a Fighter

IN THE spring of 1937, with the threat to European peace posed by the activities of Germany and Italy and the potential threat to peace in the Far East created by the expansionist aims of Japan, it became clear to the British government that the whole of Britain's defence policy was in need of review.

As far as the Royal Air Force was concerned, the overall picture was a gloomy one. At an Air Staff meeting held in January 1938, the Chief of the Air Staff pointed out that if various proposals put forward in the latest of a series of 1930s expansion schemes affecting the Service were accepted, the RAF would have only nine weeks' reserves, and if war came the full potential of the aircraft industry would not have time to develop. Among other things, the latest scheme, known as Scheme K, had recommended that planned fighter strength was to be retained at the expense of first-line bomber squadrons and reserves.

It was the Germans themselves who provided a solution to the dilemma by marching into Austria two weeks later. The British Cabinet, hitherto slow to react and still unable to agree on Britain's air defence needs, at last moved into action. Scheme K was quietly forgotten and replaced by Scheme L, which was drawn up in conditions of near panic in that same month. This envisaged the rapid expansion of the RAF's strength to 12,000 aircraft over a period of two years, should war make it necessary, with the emphasis on fighter production.

It was in September 1938, at the height of the Munich crisis, that the critically weak position of the RAF was made manifest. At that time, only 100 Hurricanes and a mere six Spitfires had as yet reached Fighter Command's operational squadrons, and although forty-two Bomber Command squadrons were mobilized, thirty of them were equipped with light and medium bombers of insufficient range to reach German targets from British bases. Worse still, a critical shortage of spares meant that less than half this force was ready for combat; reserves amounted to only ten per cent, and there was a reserve of only 200 pilots.

By August 1939, on the eve of the outbreak of war, Fighter Command's first-line strength had risen to sixteen squadrons of Hurricanes and twelve of Spitfires, a figure that would increase to twenty-nine Hurricane and nineteen Spitfire squadrons by July 1940, thanks to Herculean efforts by the British aircraft industry. Military aircraft supply was now under the control of the Ministry of Aircraft Production, created in May 1940 as the brainchild of Winston Churchill and inspired by the dynamic leadership of Lord Beaverbrook; its efforts assured the flow of fighter aircraft to the squadrons during the crucial weeks of the Battle of Britain, which in turn assured the nation's survival. Meanwhile, other factories were producing the strategic bombers which, once the air battle over Britain was won, would take the war to the enemy.

The effort was just enough to sustain Britain through her darkest time, but it was achieved at the expense of air defence requirements in the Middle East and Far East, both areas where the British Empire had the primary defensive responsibility. In each case, the most modern type in service with the RAF squadrons was the Bristol Blenheim light bomber; fighter defences rested on obsolescent types such as the Gloster Gladiator.

The clean appearance of the design was further enhanced by the use of the conical lofting method of streamlining, which involved using true circles, parabolas, ellipses and hyperbolas in establishing the basic line of each component, which could then be defined in basic algebraic terms for ease of transfer to master jigs and tools. For ease of assembly the airframe was divided into five major components – forward, centre and rear fuselage and two wing halves – all of which were fitted with their wiring and piping systems before being joined together.

The all-metal airframe featured a semi-monocoque fuselage and a twin-spar, cantilever stressed skin wing. All control surfaces were also metal skinned, and large split trailing edge flaps took up the whole of the space between ailerons and wing roots. The wide track main undercarriage retracted inwards into wells recessed into the wing leading edge; immediately aft of each wheel well was a self-sealing fuel tank with a capacity of ninety US gallons. The tail wheel was steerable and full castering, and retracted forwards into the rear fuselage. Undercarriage, flaps and brakes were hydraulically operated.

The design conference was held in a London hotel room, with February fog swirling outside, and the Air Ministry

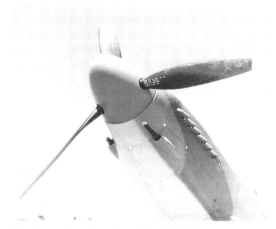

Photograph showing the 0.50 Browning gun installation in the nose of the P-51 Mustang.

representatives were enthusiastic about the concept with the exception of the proposed armament. The original North American design included an armament of either four 0.50 calibre guns or a mix of two 0.50s and two 0.30s, similar to that of the Curtiss P-50, but the Air Ministry requirement specified an eight-gun armament on a par with that fitted to the Spitfire and Hurricane. In the end an agreement was reached; the aircraft would carry eight guns, comprising two 0.50 calibre Browning MG 53 guns in the lower front fuselage beneath the engine and one in each wing just outside the propeller disc, plus two 0.30 Browning MG 40 guns in each wing, the MG 53s having 400 rounds per gun and the MG 40s 500 rpg.

Agreement was also reached on the powerplant. Early in 1940, the most powerful in-line engine available in the United States was the Allison V-1710 series of liquid-cooled V-12 powerplants. The engine selected was the Allison V-1710-F36, which drove a Curtiss three-bladed constant speed propeller of 10ft 6in diameter and was rated at 1,150 horsepower at 11,800 feet. It was an engine designed to produce optimum performance at lower and medium altitude, which was exactly what the RAF required in a tactical fighter.

With preliminary negotiations successfully concluded, North American received a Letter of Intent from the British government on 10 April 1940 and went ahead with detailed design work on the project, which was now designated NA-73X. The Letter of Intent was followed by a formal contract on 23 May, with North American predicting a completion date for the prototype in January 1941.

Work on the new fighter prototype made a tremendous impact on North American's routine in Mine Field, near Los Angeles, where the 150-strong workforce had been concentrating on production of the AT-6. Personnel in the fabrication shops worked sixteen-hour shifts, seven days a week, and the basic airframe was completed in just 102 days. Another two weeks saw the systems installed and the airframe, minus its engine

The Mustang prototype. The aircraft was given the civil registration NX19998.

AG345, the first Mustang for Britain, seen before being painted in RAF camouflage.

Mustang I AM148 RM-G of No 26 Squadron. The aircraft is flown by Pilot Officer (later Air Marshal Sir) Frederick Sowrey.

AG346 and other Mustang Is were tested in simulated combat against a captured Messerschmitt Bf 109E (RAF serial DG200) assigned to No 1426 Flight at Duxford; in this case the Mustang was the better of the two on most counts, but by this time the Bf 109E had been replaced in Luftwaffe service by the F series and the Focke-Wulf Fw 190 had also made its debut, so the results of these trials were unrealistic.

Because of its limitations as a high-altitude interceptor, it was decided to use the Mustang I as a high-speed ground attack and tactical reconnaissance fighter, at first supplementing and then replacing the P-40 Tomahawk then serving with the squadrons of Army Co-Operation Command. For this revised role an F24 oblique camera was installed aft of the cockpit on the port side of the rear fuselage and the armament was reduced to six guns, one 0.30 Browning MG 40 being deleted from each wing. The plan was to equip eighteen ACC squadrons with the new aircraft, although sixteen in fact eventually received it.

By the end of 1941 a steady stream of Mustang Is was leaving the North American factory, to be crated for shipment to England. Not all survived the hazardous Atlantic crossing; before the end of 1942 twenty-one would have been lost in passage, the victims of U-Boats or of attacks by Focke-Wulf Kondors.

Of the first few Mustang Is to arrive safely in England, three – AG356, AG360 and AG365 – were allocated to the Air Fighting Development Unit (AFDU), while AG351, AG357 and AG359 followed the second production aircraft to the A&AEE. Others, beginning with AG350, were allocated to No 41 Operational Training Unit at Old Sarum, Wiltshire, where they joined the OTU's Tomahawks and Lysanders.

More early Mustang Is were delivered singly to various Army Co-Operation Command units, notably No 4 Squadron (AG347) and No 241 Squadron (AG355). But it was another pioneer ACC squadron, No 26, that was the first to become fully equipped with the type, starting in January 1942.

Chapter 2
The Mustang I in Army Co-Operation Command, 1942–3

IN THE years between the wars, despite the advances in the use of tactical air power in the closing months of the First World War – and in particular during the Ludendorff Offensives of March-April 1918 – the RAF Air Staff tended to turn its back on the concept of army co-operation. The use of aircraft to scout for the army and to ensure rapid liaison between ground forces, especially in remote areas such as the North-West Frontier of India, was one thing; to use aircraft in an offensive role, in close support of ground forces, was quite another. Indeed, in 1937 such a role was described by the incoming Chief of the Air Staff, Sir Cyril Newall, as a 'gross misuse of air forces' – and this at a time when close support from the air was being carried out with great effect by both sides in the Spanish Civil War.

A number of factors contributed towards this lack of interest in army co-operation, not the least of which was a growing conviction in Air Staff circles that a future war could be won by a vigorous strategic bombing campaign. There was also a fear that, if the army were to exercise control over too much of the RAF's first-line strength, the point might be reached where the junior Service might lose its hard-won independent status – a status unique, in the 1930s, among all the world's air arms.

To be fair, the War Office did not help matters by making unreasonable demands. In March 1939, with a British Expeditionary Force forming for service on the Continent in the event of war, the War Office sought an allocation of one army co-operation squadron per division and one per army corps, a total of thirty-nine squadrons. But the War Office also wanted six long-range reconnaissance squadrons, twenty-four 'direct support' squadrons with aircraft performing the same close-range bombing duties as Germany's Ju 87 Stukas, which had been tried and tested in Spain, four communications squadrons and an additional number of gunnery spotting, transport and fighter squadrons. All this added up to over 100 squadrons, roughly the combined strengths of RAF Bomber and Fighter Commands.

As it was, the BEF went to France in September 1939 woefully lacking in air support. For battlefield reconnaissance and liaison there were six squadrons of Westland Lysanders, aircraft which had a limited ground attack capability but which were desperately vulnerable to light anti-aircraft fire and fighter attack; for air defence there were two squadrons of Hawker Hurricanes and two of Gloster Gladiator biplanes; while for bombing operations in the battle area there were two squadrons of Bristol Blenheims, which – as events were to prove so tragically – were also highly vulnerable in a hostile fighter environment. All the squadrons of the BEF's Air Component, including those sent to the Continent as reinforcements, were to suffer appalling losses in the Battle of France.

The sorry outcome of that campaign finally brought home to the Air Staff the need for strong, modern and effective army co-operation, and on 1 December 1940 Army Co-Operation Command was formed. Its Air Officer Commanding was Air Marshal Sir Arthur Barratt, who – as the former commander of the British Air Forces in France – had witnessed at first hand the high degree of tactical co-operation that existed between the Luftwaffe and the German ground forces.

The most pressing requirement was for a modern fighter-reconnaissance aircraft to replace the obsolete Lysander in the tactical reconnaissance role, and this immediate demand was met by the supply of fifty Curtiss P-40s by the US Government. These aircraft were diverted from a French contract placed early in 1940, before France was overrun. Designated Tomahawk MkI in RAF service, the P-40 was armed with only two .50 calibre guns with 200 rounds per gun; the first batch was delivered without armour plating protection, armoured windscreens or self-sealing fuel tanks. The other ninety P-40s of the French order, still on the Curtiss production line, had these omissions rectified at the insistence of the British, and four .30 calibre machine-guns were added to the armament. These aircraft were eventually delivered as Tomahawk IIAs.

Because of its poor armament and the inadequate altitude performance of its Allison V-1710 engine, the Tomahawk I was allocated to Army Co-Operation Command and the first examples entered service with No 26 Squadron at Gatwick in February 1941. In May 1941 No 268 Squadron at Snailwell was also equipped with Tomahawks – this time the Mk IIA version – and in June and July Nos 239 and 241 Squadrons at Gatwick and Bottisham followed suit. In August, No 2 Squadron at Sawbridgeworth and No 613 Squadron at Doncaster also received Tomahawk IIAs. In the course of 1942 four more ACC squadrons, Nos 4, 168, 171 and 231, received Tomahawks as well.

Early in 1941, the principles governing the effective use of air power in army co-operation were becoming better defined. In fact, they were broken down into three main elements, the first and most important of which was to secure intimate relations between the two Services at key points, for example at top Command level, at important field headquarters and at the battle front itself. The second element was the creation of an independent signals network, cutting out wasteful competition for signal priorities, and the third was that at certain times, army co-operation would be the function not of specialized aircraft carrying out special tasks, but of all available air power.

In 1941 these principles were already being put into increasingly effective practice in the Western Desert, where ultimately the Desert Air Force was to write a whole new textbook on close support tactics. But such tactics were evolved under the demands of battle; at home, where the only force in regular contact with the enemy was RAF Bomber Command, the application of army co-operation principles proved far more difficult, mainly because of the rigidity of the command structure. For example, Air Marshall Barratt exercised no operational control over No 71 Group, which encompassed the Command's flying squadrons; these were distributed among the larger units of the home forces, which used them as required. One problem was that, a year after the debacle of Dunkirk and with the threat of invasion removed, at least for the time being, the British Army was in the full throes of reorganizing and re-equipping. The mood was one of taking the war to the enemy as soon as possible, and that meant massive strength in manpower and materials. In the meantime, close co-ordination between the army and tactical air power remained virtually non-existent.

The result was that during 1941, the army co-operation squadrons, some of which now operated a mixture of Lysanders and Tomahawks (it would be some time before the Lysanders were withdrawn or relegated to other duties) continued in much the same way as before, their main tasks still seen as reconnaissance and artillery spotting, leading a nomadic existence as they travelled around the country in support of the various Army formations. Between May and December 1941, for example, No 268 Squadron visited no fewer than thirteen airfields, a figure that does not include flight detachments.

From October 1941, some of the Tomahawk-equipped squadrons – notably Nos 26 and 268, which had more experience on the type than the rest – were released for

Mustang I AM148 demonstrates the angular, aggressive lines of No 26 Squadron's new aircraft, early 1942. AM148 was striken off charge in April 1944.

destroyed by Pilot Officer Hollis H. Hills of No 414 Squadron. Hills was flying number two to his leader, who was attacked by the enemy fighter at low level. By an odd coincidence, Hills was a native of Los Angeles, the birthplace of the Mustang, who – like many other American pilots – had enlisted in the RCAF. It was therefore rather appropriate that to him should fall the honour of gaining the Mustang's first combat victory.

The attrition of Dieppe accounted for more than one-third of the Mustang losses – twenty-eight in total – sustained on operations during 1942. A further forty aircraft, seven of them belonging to No 41 OTU, were also lost through other causes during the year, as the following summary shows. Losses on operations are denoted by **.

41 OTU

AG350   Collided with Tomahawk AH771 while landing, Oatlands Hill, 30.5.42.

AG381   Collided with AL961 (170 Sqn) at Oatlands Hill, 16.8.42. (Note: Oatlands Hill was used for fighter recce training by the OTU. The airfield was a satellite of Old Sarum.)

AG388   Failed to recover from aerobatics near Ringwood, Hants, 26.7.42.

AG438   Collided with Fairey Fulmar N4126 ten miles north of Yeovil, 19.9.42.

AG453   Hit ground in bad visibility at Ledbury, Herefordshire, 4.12.42.

AG433   Damaged beyond repair at Speke, 3.4.42.

AG505   Hit ground in bad visibility near Molesworth, Cheshire, 20.11.42.

No 2 Squadron

AG403   Collided with AG488 on take off at Sawbridgeworth, 9.5.42 (AG488 repairable).

AG456   Pilot became lost in bad weather and abandoned A/c near Ludgershall, Buckinghamshire, 29.10.42.

AG478   Dived into ground at Castle Gate, Penzance, 28.7.42.

AG551   Flew into ground during practice strafing attack at Sturt Flat Ranges, Somerset, 30.6.42. The aircraft disintegrated on impact and the pilot was thrown clear, surviving. ('Target fixation' resulting in accidents like this was not uncommon. It happened more

Mustang I F-XU of No 2 Squadron, RAF Army Co-Operation Command.

frequently on operations, where pilots were sometimes seen to fly straight down an 'avenue' of flak coming up at them and crash into the target, having made no attempt to pull up.)

AG605 Flew into ground in bad weather, Ware, Hertfordshire, 29.10.42.

AG633 Crashed during overshoot in bad weather at Sawbridgeworth, 29.10.42.

AP164 Missing on operations, 29.11.42.**

No 4 Squadron

AG631 Suffered engine failure and crash-landed at Aldermaston, 24.11.42.

AG663 Crashed in bad weather at Sawbridgeworth, 29.10.42.

AP208 Crashed into a hill in bad weather at Dunsop Bridge, Yorkshire, 29.11.42.

No 16 Squadron

AG467 Failed to return from shipping recce off Brittany, 29.11.42.**

AG573 Crashed after engine failure on over-shoot at Harrowbeer, 23.6.42.

AG622 Failed to return from shipping recce off Brittany, 29.11.42.**

AG643 Missing after engagement with Fw 190s off the Ile de Batz, 12.12.42.**

AM115 Hit tree during tactical exercise near Frampton, Maiden Newton, Dorset, 18.10.42.

No 26 Squadron

AG399 Failed to return from armed recce, 16.7.42.**

AG415 Crashed during strafing attack on barges near Le Touquet, 14.7.42.**

AG418 Failed to return from Dieppe, 19.8.42.**

AG463 Failed to return from Dieppe, 19.8.42.**

AG532 Failed to return from recce to Abbeville, 16.7.42.**

AG536 Failed to return from Dieppe, 19.8.42.**

AL977 Failed to return from Dieppe, 19.8.42.**

AM199 Hit by flak and ditched 12 miles west of Le Touquet, 21.9.42.**

AM206 Failed to return from Doullens area after pilot reported A/c hit by flak, 27.11.42.**

AM215 Collided with AG554 during low level exercise near Wilton, Wiltshire, 26.8.42.

AG554 See above.

AG556 Overturned on landing at Gatwick, 2.12.42.

AG584 Failed to return from Dieppe, 19.8.42.

AG594 Failed to return from armed recce, Fecamp, 7.12.42.**

No 63 Squadron

AM162 Dived into ground on approach to Leeming, 2.12.42.

AM168 Spun into ground out of cloud, Preston Moor, Yorkshire, 4.10.42.

No 169 Squadron

AL983 Dived into ground at East Marden, Sussex, 15.8.42.

AL988 Hit blister hangar while low flying at Clifton, 20.12.42.

AL998 Crashed while attempting a forced landing near Church Fenton, 27.10.42.

AM241 Hit sea during low flying exercise off Isle of Man, 21.10.42.

No 170 Squadron

AL961 Hit AG381 (41 OTU) on landing at Oatlands hill, 16.8.42.

AM140 Struck high tension cable during low flying exercise near Standlake, Oxford, 13.8.42.

No 225 Squadron

AG414 Hit high tension cables during low flying exercise near Macmerry, Lothian, 1.10.42.

No 239 Squadron

AG439 Dived into ground out of low cloud, Boxley Wood, Maidstone, 30.5.42.

AG472 Failed to return from armed recce to Bruges, 14.8.42.**

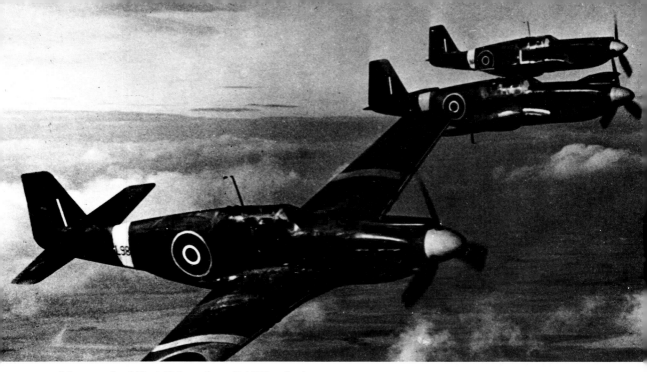

Mustang Is of No 169 Squadron, RAF Duxford.

AG524   Failed to return from armed recce to Bruges, 14.8.42.**

AG533   Shot down by flak near Fecamp, 19.8.42 (Dieppe operations).**

AG537   Failed to return from Dieppe, 19.8.42.**

AG567   Missing after engagement with Fw 190s near Caudebec, 21.7.42.**

AM134   Shot down near Le Treport (Dieppe operation) 19.8.42.**

No 241 Squadron

AG504   Flew into high ground in bad visibility five miles south of Girvan, Ayrshire, 13.9.42.

AG580   Flew into high ground in bad visibility at Heathfield, Ayrshire, 13.9.42.

No 268 Squadron

AG413   Failed to return from shipping recce off Dutch coast, 29.7.42.**

AG452   Hit fuel bowser on take off at Matlask, 11.10.42.

AG461   Failed to return from shipping recce off Dutch coast, 29.7.42.**

AG466   Crashed on take off at Snailwell, 7.7.42.

AM143   Shot down over Holland, 26.11.42.**

AP212   Shot down by flak near Petten, Holland, 7.12.42.**

No 400 Squadron, RCAF

AG540   Flew into high ground in fog near Land's End, 21.7.42.

AM151   Failed to return from Dieppe, 19.8.42.**

No 414 Squadron, RCAF

AG375   Ditched off Dieppe after engagement with Fw 190, 19.8.42.**

AG654   Crashed after engine failure on take off at Tangmere, 3.11.42.

No 613 Squadron

AG509   Struck high ground in bad weather near Settle, Yorkshire, 14.10.42.

AG586   Abandoned in bad weather near Pately Bridge, Yorkshire, 15.12.42.

AG602   Failed to return from operations, 7.12.42.**

The foregoing statistics clearly show which Mustang squadrons bore the brunt of operational flying during 1942. For other squadrons, the main task remained army co-operation in the United Kingdom. In the late summer and autumn of 1942, for example, Nos 63, 241 and 225 Squadrons were all based in Scotland, carrying out tactical exercises in co-operation with the British Army's V Corps, which had been assigned to Operation *Torch*, the forthcoming Allied landings in North Africa. At the end of October No 225 Squadron departed for the North African theatre with a mixed complement of Mustangs and Hurricane IICs; No 241 Squadron followed on 12 November, having re-equipped completely with Hurricanes.

The winter of 1942–3 was a busy period for No 268 Squadron at Snailwell in East Anglia, an airfield which the Mustangs now shared with the Typhoons of No 181 Squadron. In addition to *Lagoon* operations against enemy shipping, No 268 Squadron was becoming increasingly involved in bomber escort work, and on 22 January 1943 the Mustangs escorted North American Mitchell II bombers of No 98 Squadron, RAF West Raynham, in an attack on enemy targets in Holland. The bombers were intercepted by Fw 190s, and in the ensuing air combat No 268 Squadron destroyed an enemy fighter – its first – for the loss of two Mustangs, AM178 and AP243, the latter shot down by flak off Walcheren. No 169 Squadron from Duxford also lost two Mustangs, AL990 and AP187, during the day's operations. Both aircraft failed to return from a bomber escort mission to Ghent. On the next day, 23 January, it was the turn of No 168 Squadron at Odiham to suffer when two of its aircraft, AG510 and AG578, failed to return from an armed reconnaissance to Berck.

Apart from that, the only other Mustang loss due to enemy action in January 1943 was AG545 of No 4 Squadron, which failed to return from a reconnaissance of the Somme area on the 18th. To this total, however, must be added a further tragic loss when Mustang AG589 of No 400 Squadron RCAF was shot down in error by a Typhoon ten miles south of St Catherine's Point, Isle of Wight, as the aircraft was returning to base after a cross-Channel recce on 20 January.

There was more activity for No 268 Squadron on 12 February 1943, when seven Mustangs flew out over the North Sea to attack the SS barracks at Amersfoort in Holland. The pilots also found a Dornier Do 217 on the approach to land at Soesterberg and shot it down. Only two Mustangs were lost on operations during the month; on the 6th, AP236 of No 26 Squadron failed to return from a reconnaissance to St Valery, and on the 18th AM150 of No 63 Squadron went down into the sea some thirty-five miles off the English coast after being hit by enemy flak.

On 24 March 1943 the Typhoons of No 181 Squadron left for Gravesend to take part in cross-Channel operations, and their place at Snailwell was taken by the Mustangs of No 170 Squadron which arrived from Andover. All operations from Snailwell were under the control of No 12 Group, RAF Fighter Command.

At the end of March 1943, the biggest concentration of Mustangs was at Dunsfold in Surrey, where Nos 400, 414 and 430 Squadrons formed No 39 Army Co-Operation Wing, RCAF. All three squadrons sent frequent detachments to Middle Wallop and other locations in the south-west of England, and in March the whole wing took part in Exercise *Spartan*, the air and ground crews operating from tented encampments in the Hampshire countryside. Many other squadrons also took part in this exercise, which was designed to assess operational efficiency under mobile conditions. Throughout this period, the role of No 39 Wing remained tactical reconnaissance.

Two other Mustang squadrons involved in Exercise *Spartan* were Nos 26 and 239, which together with the Hurricane IIBs of No 175 Squadron comprised No 38 Wing, Army Co-Operation Command, based at Stoney Cross in Hampshire. The airfield was marshy and not suitable for operations by high-performance aircraft, which operated from Sommerfeld tracking (an early form of day of the month AL989 of No 169 Squadron failed to return from a coastal reconnaissance near the Pointe de Primel. No 268 Squadron lost another Mustang, AL994, on 14 May, the aircraft presumed to have been shot down by Fw 190s.

Meanwhile, Air Marshall Barratt, the AOC-in-C Army Co-Operation Command, had been drawing up a detailed report on Exercise *Spartan*, the Home Forces' exercise held in March which was, in reality, a rehearsal for the full-scale invasion and ultimate liberation of North-West Europe. The conclusions were that in the exercise, the Allies had gained marked air superiority, captured a number of airfields and were now preparing for a further advance. Barratt had recently visited North Africa to see at first hand the effects of tactical air power, and his findings confirmed the necessity for a 'composite' air force with a broader conception of air support in which the fighter, the ground attack fighter, the fighter reconnaissance aircraft, the light bomber and the heavy bomber were all harnessed for army support.

Already, on 10 March 1943, it had been decided that the so-called 'Composite Group' to support the land forces in a cross-Channel operation should be renamed a Tactical Air Force – as in Tunisia – which was to be formed within the framework of Fighter Command. This force would consist of No 2 Group (light bombers, transferred from Bomber Command); No 83 Composite Group (fighters, fighter-bombers and fighter-reconnaissance aircraft, already part of Fighter Command); No 84 Group, not yet formed; No 38 Airborne Wing, transferred from Army Co-Operation Command; and No 145 Photo-Reconnaissance Squadron.

On 1 June 1943, Army Co-Operation Command ceased to exist with the formation of the Tactical Air Force. On 10 June Air Vice-Marshal D'Albiac was appointed AOC, Tactical Air Force, and in August Air Marshal Trafford Leigh-Mallory was appointed Commander-in-Chief of the as yet non-existent Allied Expeditionary Air Force. There was little doubt that he was the

right man for the job. In 1927 he had been Commandant of the School of Army Co-Operation at Old Sarum, and had remained a staunch advocate of army co-operation principles – to the detriment, perhaps of his own career – when the higher echelons of the Air Staff were in vehement opposition to them. A controversial figure during his command of No 12 Group Fighter Command in the Battle of Britain, disliked by many, it was nevertheless Leigh-Mallory who would lay the foundations of the massive tactical air superiority that would be enjoyed by the Allies during Operation *Overlord*, the invasion of Europe, in the following year.

In that operation, and in the subsequent drive into North-West Europe, the RAF's Mustang fighters were to play a considerable part.

RAF Mustang Losses Due to Non-Operational Causes, January 1 – June 1 1943

41 OTU

AG363	Crashed at Timperley, Cheshire, after engine failure, 6.4.43.
AG400	Flew into high ground in bad weatherat Denbigh, 14.2.43.
AG502	Crashed after engine failure at low altitude, Mold, Flintshire, 28.4.43.
AG515	Collided with AP199 at low level near Whitchurch, Salop, 14.1.43.
AG585	Crashed at Hawarden after bird strike, 28.2.43.
AM183	Crashed at Gwernaffield, Flintshire, 6.5.43.
AP199	Collided with AG515 at low level near Whitchurch, Salop, 14.1.43.
AP216	Hit pole and crashed into sea at Prestatyn ranges, Flintshire, 5.2.43.
AP231	Flew into trees during low-flying exercise at Treogan, Flintshire, 14.5.43.

No 2 Squadron

AG492	Destroyed in forced landing at Burrough Grave Field, Bucks, 19.5.43.

AG550 Flew into high ground in fog at Kimmeridge, Dorset, 26.5.43.

AG623 Flew into high ground in fog at Kimmeridge, Dorset, 26.5.43.

AP210 Flew into high ground in fog at Kimmeridge, Dorset, 26.5.43.

No 4 Squadron

AG486 Crashed after engine failure at Burwell, Cambs, 10.4.43.

AG546 Crashed near Poppleton, Yorkshire, after engine failure, 20.3.43.

AG617 Dived into ground near Bellingham, Northumberland, 19.2.43.

AG647 Flew into high ground in cloud near Hillcott, Wiltshire, 9.2.43.

No 16 Squadron

AG398 Abandoned after engine failure off Anglesey, 16.5.43.

No 26 Squadron

AM171 Hit building on take off at Detling, 4.2.43.

No 63 Squadron

AM229 Hit ground during low flying exercise, Ayrshire, 25.5.43.

AP184 Crashed on take off at Macmerry, 13.5.43.

No 170 Squadron

AG485 Crashed on landing at Upavon, Wilts, 11.4.43.

AL959 Crashed in River Severn, 13.1.43.

AL968 Crashed in North Sea, 27.5.43.

AL982 Flew into sea off Selsey Bill, Sussex, 9.2.43.

AM108 Crashed during crosswind landing at Weston Zoyland, 30.5.43.

No 239 Squadron

AG614 Collided with AM136 in dummy attack near Guildford, Surrey, 17.4.43.

AM136 Collided with AG614 in dummy attack near Guildford, Surrey, 17.4.43.

No 268 Squadron

AG386 Flew into hill in bad weather at Bargrennan, Wigtown, 10.4.43.

AM142 Flew into trees during low flying exercise at Great Manderstead, Essex, 12.5.43.

No 309 Squadron

AM213 Ground-looped on landing at Peterhead, 8.5.43.

No 414 Squadron

AP185 Flew into hill in cloud near Shoreham, Sussex, 27.3.43.

No 430 Squadron

AM120 Crashed after low-altitude engine failure near Ockley, Surrey, 20.3.43.

AM255 Flew into high ground in cloud at Hindhead, Surrey, 22.4.43.

AP181 Crashed on landing at Odiham after collision with Spitfire, 19.4.43.

AP223 Hit by AG376 after landing at Dunsfold, 19.3.43.

No 613 Squadron

AG632 Flew into high ground near Brighton, Sussex, 6.2.43.

Ferry Pilots' Pool

AG471 Exploded in mid-air near Bottisham, 24.4.43.

AG566 Caught fire in the air and crashed near Ringway, 16.3.43.

Chapter 3
Into Service with the USAAF

PART OF the American government's stipulation in granting approval for the production of the Mustang for the Royal Air Force was that two aircraft were to be handed over, free of charge, for evaluation by the US Army Air Corps. These aircraft – the fourth and tenth machines of the initial production run – were flown quite intensively by AAC pilots during the second half of 1941, but no real attempt was made to evaluate them. The end of the year found both aircraft – designated XP-51s – at Wright Field, Dayton, Ohio, the US Army's principal test field for new equipment. Since the Army Air Corps was preoccupied with testing other aircraft types, the two XP-51s, much neglected, were left on the side of the field and hardly flown at all.

Meanwhile, in July 1941, Britain had ordered an additional 150 Mustangs under the terms of the Anglo-American Lend-Lease agreement. Bearing the Company designation NA-91, these differed from the earlier Mustang I in that the machine-gun armament was replaced by four wing-mounted 20mm cannon. Starting in July 1942, these aircraft were delivered to the RAF as Mustang IAs.

In the event, the RAF did not receive the whole batch, as fifty-seven were repossessed by the US Army Air Force, as the Army Air Corps had now become. Before that, Dutch Kindelberger and his design team, concerned by the lack of American interest in the Mustang as a fighter, had carried out a number of modifications to the basic design and had offered the aircraft to the US Army as a dive-bomber. The modified aircraft had a 1,325 horsepower Allison V-1710-87 engine and was fitted with powerful wing dive

The cannon-armed NA-91, which was delivered to the RAF as the Mustang Mk 1A.

The first A-36 attack bomber, flown by NAA test pilot Bob Chilton on 21 September 1942.

A-36, pictured in North Africa, early 1943.

brakes. Built-in armament was six .50 machine guns, and there was provision for two 500 pound bombs or fuel tanks on underwing pylons. The US Army was impressed by the idea, and placed a contract for 500 of the new machines for use

A-36A of the 27th Fighter Bomber Group, Tunisia, 1943.

as close support dive-bombers under the designation A-36A.

The uprated Allison engine gave the A-36A a maximum speed, clean, of 356 mph; with bombs or fuel tanks this was reduced to 310 mph at 5,000 feet. The dive-bombing performance was impressive, the aircraft achieving a consistently high degree of accuracy at an optimum diving angle of seventy degrees, the air brakes holding it to a speed of about 250 mph. Deliveries began in September 1942.

Of the fifty-seven Mustangs repossessed by the USAAF from the RAF's Mk IA contract, fifty-five were fitted with two F24 oblique cameras in the rear fuselage and were issued to the 111th and 154th Observation Squadrons of the 68th Observation Group. They initially carried the designation P-51, although this was later changed to F-6A in keeping with the aircraft's reconnaissance role. The 68 OG was assigned to the North African Theatre of Operations, and on 9 April 1943 Lt Alfred Schwab of the 154th OS became the first USAAF pilot to fly a Mustang sortie when

he took off from Tunisia on an armed reconnaissance over the Mediterranean. For a short time, the P-51 and the A-36A were known respectively – and unofficially – as 'Apache' and 'Invader' in USAAF service before the name 'Mustang' was adopted for all variants.

One point of interest is that in April and May 1943, No 225 Squadron, operating Mustang Is in North Africa, 'borrowed' a number of P-51s from the 68th OG for tactical reconnaissance and bomber escort duties. Six A-36As were similarly loaned to No 1437 Strategic Reconnaissance Flight, RAF, which operated them from Tunisia and later from Malta.

The service debut of the P-51 was followed by a USAAF contract for the production of a further 310 aircraft designated P-51As. These were fitted with the Allison V-1710-81 engine rated at 1,125 horsepower at 18,000 feet. Armament was reduced to four wing-mounted .50 calibre machine guns, two with 280 rounds per gun and two with 350, and external ordnance was the same as that of the A-36A.

The P-51A was the last Allison-powered Mustang variant.

Deliveries began in March 1943, fifty aircraft going to the RAF as Mustang IIs in part replacement for the fifty-seven repossessed P-51s. In addition, thirty-five aircraft were converted to the fighter-reconnaissance role under the designation F-6B, with the same camera installation as the F-6A.

The P-51A was the last Allison-powered Mustang variant. By the time the Tunisian Campaign drew to a close in May 1943, developments were under way that would turn the Mustang into one of the most formidable fighter aircraft of all time.

Those developments began in April 1942, just as the Mustang Mk I was entering service with the RAF. At the end of that month, Ronald W. Harker, a Rolls-Royce test pilot who was also responsible for Service liaison with the assessment of aircraft powered by other than Rolls-Royce engines, was invited by Wing Commander Ian Campbell-Orde, commanding the Air Fighting Development Unit at Duxford, to make a familiarisation flight in one of the early Mk Is. Harker's thirty-minute flight left him in no doubt that the Mustang was a first-rate aircraft up to medium altitudes,

but like others before him he was disappointed by the output of the Allison engine at higher altitudes.

It seemed obvious to Harker that far better results might be obtained by installing a Rolls-Royce Merlin engine in the Mustang airframe. The latest Merlin variant was the 61 series, production of which had been accelerated following the appearance of the Focke-Wulf Fw 190 with the *Jagdgeschwader* in France. In April 1942 100 Spitfire Mk VC airframes were hurriedly being fitted with the new powerplant, these aircraft being delivered to the hard-pressed squadrons of Fighter Command under the designation of Spitfire Mk IX.

Harker took the idea back to Rolls-Royce, where preliminary calculations suggested that a Merlin-powered Mustang would be capable of a maximum speed of 441 mph at 25,500 feet. Even if this proved to be somewhat over-optimistic (which it was), the projected performance improvement over the Allison-powered Mustang was still sufficiently impressive to stimulate the interest of some – but not all – of the senior staff at Rolls-Royce. Harker persisted, and found a valuable ally in Ray Dorey, who

Flight of two P-51As. The aircraft are carrying underwing containers for laying smoke screens.

P-51A 'Slick Chick' was a Wright Field test aircraft. It carried no weapons and remained uncamouflaged.

was in charge of the Rolls engine flight-test section at Hucknall; it was Dorey who advised him to seek an interview with E.W. (later Lord) Hives, director and general works manager of Rolls-Royce Ltd. The meeting was fruitful; Hives acted quickly and put the proposal to Air Chief Marshal Sir Wilfrid Freeman, the Air Member for Production and Research, who immediately arranged for three Mustang Mk Is to be sent to Hucknall for Merlin conversion. The contract specified that the aircraft were to be fitted with the Merlin 65 engine; this had modified supercharger gear ratios, reducing the full throttle altitude in full supercharge gear to 21,000 feet, and a higher maximum power output than the Merlin 61 thanks to the use of a Bendix-Stromberg fuel injector.

The Rolls-Royce Merlin engine installation in the Mustang.

The thinking behind the adoption of the Merlin 65 was that most Mustang operations over the Continent would be flown in the medium altitude band between 10,000 and 20,000 feet, the Spitfire IX taking care of operations at higher altitudes.

The first Mustang to be fitted with a Merlin was AL975, an Air Fighting Development Unit aircraft which, redesignated Mustang Mk X, flew for the first time in its new configuration on 13 October 1942 in the hands of Captain R.T. Shepherd, Rolls-Royce's Chief Test Pilot. The Merlin 65 engine was rated at 1,705 horsepower at 5,750 feet and initially drove a four-blade Rotol propeller of 10ft 9in diameter, as fitted to the Spitfire Mk IX, but after six flights this was replaced by an 11ft 4in propeller which had been specifically designed for the Mustang.

The second Mustang X conversion, AL963, flew on 13 November, and the third, AM121, on 13 December. Two more Mustangs, AM203 and AM208, were also converted, flying on 21 January and 7 February 1943 respectively. All five conversions were initially fitted with the Merlin 65, but AL975 later flew with the high-altitude Merlin 70 and 71 engines and AM203 was used for development testing of the Merlin 100 series.

By the end of 1942, AL963, under test at the A&AEE Boscombe Down, had attained a maximum speed in full supercharge gear of 433 mph at 22,000 feet, and in moderate supercharge gear 406 mph at 10,000 feet, both speeds at a gross weight of 9,100 pounds. Comparative figures for an Allison-engined P-51, tested by Rolls-Royce at Hucknall, were 350 and 351 mph at a gross weight of 8,620 pounds. Comparative rates of climb at sea level of the Mustang X and the P-51 (shown in parentheses) were 3,440 ft/min (1,900 ft/min), and an optimum rate of climb of 3,560 ft/min at 7,500 feet (2,000 ft/min at 11,000 feet).

While the Mustang X conversions were in progress at Hucknall, Lieutenant-Colonel Thomas Hitchcock, the US Air Attaché in London and a strong supporter of the Merlin modification, had reported the success of the scheme to USAAF and North American officials. Dutch Kindelberger, who had never really liked the combination of Mustang and Allison engine, was immediately enthusiastic about the idea. The production of Allison-powered Mustangs was drawing to a close, and the Merlin would give the design a new lease of life. Packard Motors had already been producing Merlins in the USA for about a year under licence, in order to provide stocks of the engine for Canadian-built Lancasters and other types, and so supply of the engine to power the Mustang would not present a problem. On 25 July 1942, therefore, the USAAF contracted with North American for the installation of Packard Merlins, designated V-1650-3s in the USA, in two Mustang P-51-NA airframes, 41-37352 and 41-37421.

The first of these two conversions, both still retaining their four-cannon armament, flew on 30 November 1942 at Inglewood. Because of numerous design changes associated with the Merlin engine the aircraft was originally designated XP-78, but this was later changed to XP-51B. Modifications included the relocation of the carburettor air intake under the nose, as in the British Merlin-Mustang, the positioning of the supercharger intercooler within the ventral radiator to reduce drag, the strengthening of the airframe to accommodate the uprated engine and the fitting of new ailerons. The P-51B prototypes were fitted with four-blade Hamilton Standard Hydromatic propellers of 11ft 2in diameter. It was decided that the armament of production aircraft would be either four or six .50 Brownings.

Even before the XP-51B flew, General H.H. Arnold, the Commanding General, USAAF, had become convinced of the Merlin-Mustang's enormous potential and had placed orders on behalf of the Army for some 2,000 of the new aircraft. To accommodate the massive increase in production, North American set up two new plants, one at Dallas, Texas, and the

The Merlin-engined XP-51B Mustang.

P-51B Mustang displaying wing leading edge patches where the 20 mm cannon have been removed.

other at Tulsa, Oklahoma. Mustangs produced at Dallas received the designation P-51C, although they were virtually identical to the P-51B.

Testing and evaluation of the P-51B revealed that the aircraft actually had a better performance than had been predicted. Moreover, the strengthened wing meant that it was able to carry two 1,000 pound bombs or a pair of drop tanks. Later production P-51B/Cs were also fitted with a fuselage fuel tank having a capacity of eighty-five US gallons, and this, together with the two seventy-five US gallon drop tanks, gave the aircraft a maximum range of 1,240 miles. Range on internal fuel only was 815 miles.

The report produced by the Army Air Forces Board enthused about the qualities of the P-51B in comparison with other American fighter types:

'The P-51B, from sea level to 11,000 ft, is some seven to ten miles per hour slower than the P-51A which is the fastest fighter at this altitude. Between 14,000 and 22,000 ft, the P-51B is about fifteen to twenty mph faster. From 22,000 ft the P-51B, in high blower, widens this speed advantage up to seventy-five mph at 30,000 ft.

'From sea level, the P-51B gradually gains on the P-38J and the P-47D until, at 16,000 ft, it has a speed of about 420 mph which is about ten mph faster than the P-38J and about twenty mph faster than the P-47D. Above 27,000 ft, the P-51B can no longer get war emergency power, but its speed of about 430 mph at 30,000 ft is equal to that of the P-47D and about twenty mph faster than the P-38J, both using war emergency power. The P-51B is capable of 400 mph at 40,000 ft.

'The P-51B is by far the best climbing aircraft of all current American fighters. It takes about 4.5 minutes to get to 15,000 ft as against five minutes for the P-38J and about seven minutes for the P-47J. The P-51B maintains a lead of about .5 minute over the P-38J to 30,000 ft and reaches that altitude in about eleven minutes which is about 6.5 minutes faster than the P-47D.

'In zooming the P-51B with the P-47D from level flight at cruising and high speeds, and from high speeds out of dives, the P-51B gains speed rapidly and leaves the P-47D far behind. In zooming the P-51B with the P-38J, from level flight at cruising speed, the fighters climb evenly at the start. However, the P-51B falls off while the P-38B keeps climbing. In zooms from high speeds (425 indicated air speed) the P-51B pulls away from the P-38J and it soon ends considerably higher.

'The diving characteristics of the P-51B are superior to those of any other fighter plane. It is exceptionally easy to handle and requires very little trimming. The P-51B dives away from all other fighters except the P-47D, against which the P-51B loses several hundred feet ahead in the initial pushover and then holds that position, apparently neither gaining nor losing distance.

'The new seal-balanced ailerons of the P-51B give the fighter a faster rate of roll at all speeds than any other fighter except the P-47D with which it is equal at cruising speeds.

'The search view of the P-51B is better than in the P-51A but is still obstructed above, to both sides, and to the rear, by the canopy construction. The view forward over the nose is considerably improved over the P-51A by the relocation of the carburetor air intake scoop, the elimination of the clear view panel on the left side of the windshield, and lowering of the nose of the engine one and one-half degrees.

'The fighting qualities of the P-51B were compared with those of the P-47D-10 and the P-38J-5 and, briefly, with the P-39N-0 and the P-40N. The only maneuver the P-39 and P-40 have that is superior to the P-51B is a slight advantage in a turning circle. In all other maneuvers, as well as performance, they are both far inferior. The P-51B has good performance at all altitudes, but above 20,000 ft the performance improves rapidly, and its best fighting altitude is between 25 and 35,000 ft. The rate of climb is outstanding, with an average of about 3,000 ft per minute from sea level to 25,000 ft. Above 20,000 ft, the overall fighting qualities of this aircraft are superior to those of all the other types used in the trials.'

P-51B Mustang FB108, bearing US insignia, RAF fin flash and British serial. This aircraft served with No 129 Squadron RAF and was lost near Vire, France, in June 1944.

P-51B FX883, also in dual markings, was diverted from the RAF order and assigned to the USAAF in December 1943.

The Merlin-engined Mustang had proved itself beyond all doubt; the priority now was to get the fighter into operational service as quickly as possible, an aim that was temporarily thwarted by an initial slow delivery of Packard-built Merlins.

The most pressing need for the P-51B was in the European Theatre. In June 1943 the Combined Chiefs of Staff issued their directive for the start of Operation *Pointblank*, the joint round-the-clock Anglo-American bombing offensive against Germany's war industries. In terms of offensive power the US Eighth Air Force was well equipped to undertake such an operation: by the beginning of July its strength in the British Isles had increased to fifteen bomber groups comprising more than 300 B-17s and B-24s. The biggest obstacle to deep-penetration daylight missions, as operations during the first half of the year had revealed, remained the lack of long-range fighter escort. In an effort to fill this critical gap the Americans provided their P-38 Lightnings and P-47 Thunderbolts with drop tanks, which

enabled them to penetrate as far as Germany's western frontier, but this did not provide a real solution. The first mission by P-47s with drop tanks, flown on 28 July, was a success, but it was not long before the German fighter leaders developed new combat techniques that went a long way towards eliminating the Americans' advantage. The enemy fighters would attack the P-47s as they crossed the Dutch coast, forcing them to jettison their auxiliary tanks to increase manoeuvrability.

During the last week of July 1943 the Eighth Air Force made five major sorties against sixteen targets, and in the course of these operations Eighth Bomber Command lost eighty-eight aircraft, mostly B-17s. During a follow-on three-day series of attacks against German aircraft factories forty-four more B-17s failed to return, and there was worse to come. On 17 August, in a dual attack on the Messerschmitt aircraft factory at Regensburg and ball-bearing factories at Schweinfurt, Eighth Bomber Command lost sixty out of 376 bombers despatched, sixteen per cent of the total force. Many more got home with such severe battle damage that they had to be written off.

This disaster caused Eighth Bomber Command to conserve its strength for several weeks, during which attacks were carried out only against those targets within range of fighter cover. However, Lieutenant-General Ira Eaker, the Commanding General, Eighth Bomber Command, was determined to continue with the long-range daylight offensive, and early in October the Americans were able to resume their deep penetration raids. When the attacks did start again, the lessons of August were rammed home even more forcibly. During one week between 8 and 14 October, when the Americans attacked Bremen, Marienburg, Danzig, Münster and once again Schweinfurt, they lost 148 bombers and nearly 1,500 aircrew. In the raid on Schweinfurt on 14 October, which came to be called Black Thursday, the *Luftwaffe* flew over 500 sorties and destroyed sixty of the 280 bombers taking part, more than twenty per cent.

With the Eighth Air Force reeling from this succession of disasters and RAF Bomber Command beginning to suffer increasingly heavy losses at the hands of a greatly improved German night-fighter force, the prospect for the combined Allied air offensive looked grim. The need for a long-range escort fighter was now desperate – and yet when the first P-51Bs arrived in the United Kingdom they were assigned not to the Eighth Air Force, which needed them so urgently, but to the Ninth Air Force, which had been formed for tactical operations in support of US ground forces in the planned invasion of occupied Europe.

The first unit selected to operate the P-51B in England was the 354th Fighter Group, comprising the 353rd, 355th and 356th Fighter Squadrons with an establishment of about fifty pilots under the command of Lt Col Kenneth R. Martin. The Group had formed a year earlier and trained on Bell P-39s in the United States before eventually taking ship for England, minus their aircraft.

The Group's personnel arrived in the UK on 20 October 1943 and were sent to

43-7116, one of the first production batch of P-51Bs.

Luftwaffe Intelligence was keen to learn as much as possible about the Mustang. This captured P-51B, coded T9+HK, was flown intensively at Oranienburg, near Berlin.

Greenham Common in Berkshire, which had been handed over to the Americans at the end of September and which was now known as USAAF Station 486 – to await their Mustangs, which arrived on 11 November. Meanwhile, the Eighth Air Force's leadership had been exerting pressure to have the P-51B assigned to them for escort duties; as the Ninth Air Force was still very much in an embryo state this was agreed, and after only two days at Greenham Common the 354th FG was transferred to Boxted in Essex in support of Eighth Bomber Command, although the unit remained under Ninth Air Force control.

The Group spent the last two weeks of November acclimatising itself to the new aircraft, and when General Brereton, commanding the Ninth Air Force, visited the airfield on the last day of the month he was informed that the Group would shortly be going into action. In fact the first operational sortie was flown in the afternoon of 1 December 1943, when twenty-four P-51Bs carried out a familiarisation flight along the Belgian coast as far as the Pas de Calais. One aircraft was damaged by flak. Because of the inexperience of the 354th FG's pilots, this mission was led by Major Don Blakeslee of the 4th Fighter Group from Debden, flying a P-47. Blakeslee, one of VIIIth Fighter Command's old hands, had already established his reputation as a fine fighter leader and exponent of fighter tactics. On this occasion, Lt Col Martin flew as Blakeslee's wingman.

The 354th FG flew its second operational mission on 5 December a B-17 escort to the Amiens area. No enemy aircraft were encountered, and all the P-51Bs returned safely to base. Some enemy fighters were encountered on the next mission, a bomber escort to Emden, but no claims were registered by either side. One P-51B, however, failed to return to Boxted; it was believed that technical trouble had been the cause.

On 13 December the 354th FG flew the longest fighter mission of the war up to that date when the Mustangs, operating in conjunction with the P-38s of the 55th Fighter Group from Nuthampstead, escorted B-17s to Kiel and back, a round trip of 1,000 miles. For pilots who had been flying their new aircraft for barely a month, it was a notable achievement. On 16 December the Mustangs once again penetrated deep into Germany on an escort mission to Bremen, and it was on this raid that the Group's first enemy aircraft, a Messerschmitt Bf110, was shot down by Lt Charles F. Gumm of the 355th Squadron. The success was marred by the loss of Major Owen M. Seaman, the commander of the 353rd Squadron, who disappeared without trace over the North Sea. Again, mechanical trouble was suspected. Four days later, also in the Bremen area, the Group shot down four rocket-carrying Bf110s, but three of its pilots failed to return; no-one had seen them shot down, and yet again the losses were attributed to mechanical causes.

Gradually, the pilots of the 354th FG were facing up to the problems of flying long missions of four or five hours' duration. There were bound to be technical problems, ranging from oxygen starvation to the freezing of oil and lubricants, and one by one they were met and overcome. Coolant losses at high altitude were a big problem, because the engines soon overheated and

eventually seized; fouled plugs were another, until pilots and ground crews worked out that they could be cleaned by applying bursts of power at fifteen-minute intervals. Ammunition belts had a tendency to jam the machine guns during high-G manoeuvres, but small local modifications cured that too, and were incorporated in subsequent production aircraft.

The 354th FG flew its tenth mission on 31 December 1943. By that time its pilots had shot down eight enemy aircraft for the loss of eight Mustangs, most of the latter through technical troubles. It was not an encouraging start, and the pilots were frustrated by the technical problems; the constant jamming of the guns, for example, meant that pilots were restricted to opening fire in level flight, an enormous obstacle in fighter-versus-fighter combat. For the P-51B, which had an armament of only four .50-calibre guns, the loss of even one gun through a stoppage was highly dangerous.

Nevertheless, the 354th's pilots entered the new year of 1944 determined to improve matters, and their big chance came on 5 January, during a bomber escort mission to Kiel. The bomber formation was attacked

Escort fighter's eye view: dramatic shot of a B-17 formation over Bremen, December 1943.

by a large number of Messerschmitt 110s and Focke-Wulf 190s, and in the ensuing air battle the Americans claimed the destruction of eighteen enemy aircraft for no loss.

The *Luftwaffe* was also up in strength on 11 January, when the 354th FG escorted B-17s to Aschersleben. Forty-four Mustangs were airborne on this operation, and made contact with several enemy fighter formations. The American pilots claimed the destruction of fifteen enemy aircraft, with eight probables and sixteen damaged, for no loss to themselves. The mission also resulted in the award of the Congressional Medal of Honor to the commander of the 356th Fighter Squadron, Major James H. Howard, for a particularly gallant action in which he engaged several enemy fighters single-handed, destroying three and damaging three more – all Bf110s – despite the fact that all but one of his guns jammed during the combat. Howard was a highly experienced pilot, having flown against the Japanese with the American Volunteer Group in China. He was the only British-based American fighter pilot to win the highest US decoration for valour during the Second World War.

On 24 January the Group lost two Mustangs, one flown by Captain Robert Priser, commanding the 353rd Fighter Squadron, and on 8 February three more Mustangs were shot down. In these two operations the Group could claim only one probable and one damaged. The situation was redressed on 10 February, when the Group destroyed eight enemy aircraft on an escort mission to Brunswick, and the next day the Group fought its way through strong opposition to Frankfurt, claiming fourteen enemy aircraft for the loss of two of their own number. One of the latter was the newly-promoted Group Commander, Colonel Kenneth Martin, who collided with a Bf110. Despite serious injuries he managed to bale out and survived to spend the rest of the war in prison camp. Four of the 354th FG's pilots – Lieutenants Gumm, Bradley, Turner and Beerbower – were now

aces, with five or more enemy aircraft to their credit.

Operations so far had clearly shown that one Mustang group was not enough to bring about a dramatic reduction in the losses suffered by the heavy bombers, and in the first weeks of 1944, with Eighth Bomber Command committed to the battle on a bigger scale than ever before, these once again assumed alarming proportions. Of the 238 bombers that struck at the fighter production factories at Aschersleben on 11 January, for example, sixty failed to return. But there was to be no respite; the top priority at the outset of 1944 was the destruction of the *Luftwaffe*, and it had to be achieved within a limited period as an essential prelude to the projected Allied invasion of Europe. 'Destroy the Enemy Air Force wherever you find them, in the air, on the ground and in the factories.' Such was the New Year directive that went out to all Commands from the USAAF Chief of Staff, General Arnold.

By this time, a second Mustang Group was under training in England. This, like the 354th FG, was assigned to the Ninth Air Force, but was released to the operational control of the Eighth Air Force when the latter agreed to assign a P-47 Group, the 358th FG, for service with the Ninth AF. The new Group, the 357th FG – some of whose pilots had flown occasional missions with the 354th FG – began operations from Leiston in Suffolk with a fighter sweep to Rouen on 11 February 1944, the mission being led by Jim Howard of the 354th.

The strategic air offensive against the resources of the *Luftwaffe*, code-named Operation *Argument*, presented Eighth Bomber Command with a formidable task. The events of 11 January were proof enough that the *Luftwaffe* was capable of opposing the bombers with unprecedented ferocity. Undeterred, on 20 February the Eighth Air Force launched what was at that time the biggest strategic air attack in history against several key aircraft factories in central Germany between Leipzig and Brunswick, with a massive

P-51B fitted with tubes for 3-in HVARS. These rockets later became standard ordnance for ground-attack work.

armada of 941 bombers and 700 fighters crossing the Channel. The Americans had anticipated fierce opposition and correspondingly heavy losses, but although the *Luftwaffe* committed every available fighter to the battle the Allied fighter escort prevented a high proportion from getting through to the bombers. All the target factories were hit, some of them badly, and twenty-one B-17s and B-24s failed to return. On this occasion the Mustangs of the 354th FG, led by Lt Col Howard, made their longest penetration so far, a 1,100-mile round trip to Leipzig, the pilots claiming sixteen enemy aircraft destroyed for no loss.

There was now considerable rivalry between the P-51 and P-47 fighter groups, and the fact that on more than one occasion Mustangs returned to base with battle damage caused by Thunderbolt pilots after being mistaken for Messerschmitt 109s seemed to intensify it. The Mustang's resemblance to the German fighter created constant identification problems and resulted in some tragic losses; in an attempt

to remedy matters white recognition bands were painted on the wings and tail surfaces, but the problem persisted until the P-51B/C was eventually replaced by the P-51D, with its distinctive raised, clear-vision cockpit canopy.

The rivalry was particularly keen between the 354th and Lt Col Hubert Zemke's 56th P-47 'Wolfpack' Fighter Group. In the summer of 1943, Zemke's pilots had claimed the destruction of 100 German aircraft in eighty-six days. Early in 1944 the 354th went all out to better this score, but on 21 February – their 83rd day of operations – the tally of the Mustang pilots stood at ninety-two enemy aircraft destroyed. By nightfall that same day, however, the 354th score had risen to 103, and the following day twelve more enemy aircraft were added during an escort mission to Aschersleben.

Mustang operations on 22 February were flown in support of an attack by B-17s and B-24s on aircraft factories in central Germany, the Eighth Air Force operating in concert with bombers of General Nathan F.

Twining's Fifteenth Air Force from Italy. While the latter set out to strike at the Messerschmitt aircraft factory at Regensburg from the south, Eighth Bomber Command again left its English bases to hit the factories in central Germany, as well as Gotha and Schweinfurt.

It was a bold attempt to crush the enemy defences between the jaws of a mighty pincer, but it was dogged by ill-luck right from the start. To begin with, the Eighth's English bases were covered by a dense layer of cloud, and several bombers collided as they climbed up through it. The carefully laid plans for the assembly of the bomber force over eastern England were completely dislocated. Combat Wings were scattered all over the sky, and as a result two whole Bombardment Divisions, the 2nd and 3rd, were ordered to abort and return to their fields. Only the 1st Division set course over the sea, and by this time the German coastal radar, which had been monitoring the movements of the bombers for some time, had fully alerted the *Luftwaffe* fighter *Gruppen*.

As the bombers crossed the German frontier they were attacked by over 100 fighters. The onslaught took the Americans completely by surprise. During previous attacks the Germans had concentrated their fighter defences in the immediate vicinity of the target, but now they were attacking much further to the west. They found the bombers escorted by only a handful of Thunderbolts; the Mustangs were not due to rendezvous with the bombers until the latter were approaching the target area. What followed was a massacre. The German fighters attacked again and again, and the wrecks of forty-four B-17s and B-24s lay scattered over a broad swathe of German territory from the Rhineland to the Harz Mountains. Only ninety-nine out of the original force of 430 bombers that set out actually reached their primary targets, and only two of these targets were damaged. In the south the Fifteenth Air Force successfully attacked the Messerschmitt factory at Regensburg, but they were strongly opposed by fighters of the *Luftwaffe*'s 7th

'Lucky Leaky II' was a 353rd Fighter Group P-51C. Photograph shows the aircraft, fitted with a Malcolm-type hood, after belly landing at Raydon on 2 May 1945.

P-51B Mustang of the 359th Fighter Group. The aircraft has suffered flak damage to its tail fin.

Air Division and fourteen bombers were shot down.

The *Luftwaffe* fighters were not the only ones to have changed their tactics. During early bomber escort operations in December and January, the Mustangs had been ordered to stay close to the bombers they were escorting, a highly restrictive practice that robbed the pilots of much tactical advantage. (The *Luftwaffe* fighters had been instructed by Hermann Göring to follow the same procedure during the latter stages of the Battle of Britain, with detrimental results). On 6 January 1944, however, command of the Eighth Air Force was assumed by General James Doolittle, who was quick to appreciate the close escort problem. He changed the orders, and from then on the Mustangs were free to sweep ahead of the bombers, engaging the enemy fighters before the latter were in an attacking position.

During the last week of February 1944 a third P-51B fighter group, the 363rd FG, became operational at Rivenhall in Essex, beginning operations on the 23rd. On 25 February favourable weather conditions

extended over the whole of Germany, and the Strategic Air Forces launched over 800 bombers in a massive assault on the Messerschmitt aircraft factories at Regensburg and Augsburg from the south and west. As the two bomber streams approached Regensburg from these two different points of the compass, the officer commanding 7 *Fliegerdivision*, General Huth, was faced with a difficult decision. He did not have enough fighters to deal with both enemy forces; the question was, which stream to concentrate on? In the end he decided to throw most of his *Gruppen* against the southern stream, consisting of 176 bombers. It was a wise choice; the Allied fighter escort was absent, and thirty-three bombers were shot down.

The bomber stream from the west, on the other hand, was escorted by all three Mustang fighter groups, and they soon began to make their presence felt. On this occasion comparatively few enemy fighters managed to break through the strong fighter screen. Those that did, together with the flak, accounted for thirty-one out of a total force of 738

Fortresses and Liberators. The overall loss of sixty-four heavy bombers during the day's operations was not light, but the damage they inflicted on the aircraft factories was enormous: at Regensburg the Messerschmitt works was practically levelled.

Although in the final analysis the so-called 'Big Week' offensive made little difference to the output of single-seat fighters for the *Luftwaffe*, which reached the level of 2,000 per month by the middle of 1944, the daylight offensive of January-April 1944 cost the *Luftwaffe* more than 1,000 pilots, many of them veteran fighter leaders. Although the claims of the Fortress and Liberator gunners were vastly inflated in the confusion of air battle, there was no escaping the fact that the *Luftwaffe* lost an average of fifty pilots every time the Americans mounted a major raid. The Allied fighter escort, and particularly the Mustangs, began to account for more enemy aircraft with every passing week.

In February 1944 Don Blakeslee's 4th Fighter Group at Debden had also begun converting to the P-51B, the first three aircraft arriving on the 14th. These were assigned to each of the Group's three squadrons, the 334th, the 335th and 336th, and conversion went ahead while the Group continued to operate its P-47s. The 4th FG had completely re-equipped with Mustangs by the beginning of March and was declared fully operational, although many of the pilots had as little as one hour's flying time on the new aircraft.

On 3 March 1944 Blakeslee was selected to lead his group to Berlin, but the honour of being the first commander to take fighters over the enemy capital was to elude him. The large force of 748 bombers and their escorts got as far a Schleswig-Holstein when they were recalled because of deteriorating weather; on the way home the 4th encountered a large formation of enemy fighters, and in the ensuing battle lost four Mustangs against five kills. Meanwhile, the P-38 Lightnings of the 55th Fighter Group

from Wormingford, in Essex, led by Lt Col Jack Jenkins, had not heard the recall and continued on to Berlin. It was only after they returned to base, freezing cold and fed up with long hours battling through the bad weather, that they realised they had become famous. For once, the Mustangs had been overshadowed.

The Berlin mission was re-scheduled for the next day, with 770 fighters, including five groups drawn from the Ninth Air Force, escorting 500 Fortresses and Liberators. Once again, Don Blakeslee had the task of leading the fighter escort. Once again the mission was frustrated by poor weather, and a mere twenty-nine bombers reached the enemy capital, as did the 4th, 354th and 357th Fighter Groups. Other groups encountered strong fighter opposition over the Netherlands and the Americans lost twenty-three fighters, the Ninth Air Force's 363rd Group losing eleven Mustangs after being bounced by enemy fighters near Hamburg.

When the Eighth Air Force mounted another major attack on Berlin on 6 March, the Americans encountered revised German fighter tactics. The *Luftwaffe* now sent up its aircraft in formations of *Geschwader* strength – sixty to eighty fighters – with one of the three *Gruppen* earmarked to attack the bombers while the other two strove to keep the Mustangs at bay. Some of the Messerschmitt 109G *Gruppen* now had aircraft fitted with the Daimler-Benz DG605AS high-altitude engine, which gave them an altitude advantage over the P-51B, and the Mustang pilots often found themselves with a tough fight on their hands. Nevertheless, the German fighters suffered an appalling rate of attrition; in the battles that raged over Berlin on 6 March the Americans lost sixty-nine bombers and eleven fighters, but the *Luftwaffe* lost eighty aircraft, some forty per cent of the defending fighter force.

During March 1944 Don Blakeslee's 4th Fighter Group alone claimed 156 enemy aircraft destroyed, and as the month wore on the German defences became noticeably weaker. Another attack on Berlin by 590 bombers, escorted by 801 fighters on 8 March, when several key factories were destroyed, cost the Americans thirty-seven bombers and seventeen fighters, but when 669 bombers again struck at the capital on the 22nd they encountered almost no opposition. Twelve bombers were shot down, but all of them were victims of the flak.

In the south too, the *Luftwaffe* was being steadily decimated. On 16 March a force of heavy bombers sent out to attack Augsburg was intercepted by forty-three Messerschmitt 110s of ZG 76. Their rockets accounted for five bombers, but then the Mustang escort pounced and destroyed twenty-six 110s. For Messerschmitt's elderly 'destroyer', which had fought its way through the war from the beginning in Poland, it was the end. It was withdrawn from the daylight air defence role and replaced by the more modern Messerschmitt 410.

In the spring of 1944 five more fighter groups converted to the P-51B/C in the Eighth Air Force. These were the 339th FG at Fowlmere, Cambridgeshire; the 352nd FG at Bodney, Norfolk; the 355th at Steeple Morden, Cambridgeshire; the 359th at East Wretham, Norfolk; and the 361st at Bottisham, Cambridgeshire. The first four were all operational by the end of April 1944, the 361st FG following in May.

The increase in the number of operational Mustang groups was accompanied by a revision of tactics. Although bomber escort remained the main priority, some Mustang units, particularly those in the Ninth Air Force, were authorised to attack ground targets from late March 1944. This work was pioneered by the 354th FG, which on 26 March attacked the marshalling yards and adjacent airfield at Creil, each Mustang carrying a pair of 500 pound bombs. On 5 April, the 4th and 355th FG attacked airfields in the Berlin and Munich areas, claiming a collective total of forty-three enemy aircraft destroyed on the ground and ten more in air combat. It was a dangerous and exacting role, but one in which the P-51 was to excel in the months to come, as the weight of the Allied air forces turned to the support of the invasion of Normandy.

Chapter 4
RAF Mustang Operations to D-Day, 6 June 1944

OF THE seventeen Mustang squadrons on the RAF Order of Battle in the United Kingdom at the formation of the Tactical Air Force in June 1943, two, Nos 26 and 516, were to be exclusively engaged in Army co-operation work during the second half of the year, assisting the ground forces in training for the forthcoming invasion of Europe. During most of this period No 26 Squadron operated from Church Fenton in Yorkshire, while No 516 remained based at Dundonald in Scotland.

Two more, Nos 169 and 170 Squadrons, were assigned mainly to air defence duties, operating from a number of airfields in

continued to fly armed reconnaissance sorties as required, losing three Mustangs on operations. AL981 of No 170 Squadron failed to return from a shipping reconnaissance off Les Sept Isles on 26 July, and the squadron also lost AG417 during a TacR sortie to Evreux airfield on 6 August 1943. AP189 of No 169 Squadron was also shot down by flak near Morlaix on that day. No 169 Squadron disbanded on 30 September 1943, being reformed at Ayr the next day as a night-fighter squadron for operations in No 100 (Countermeasures) Group. No 170 Squadron also disbanded in January 1944, reforming in October that

AL975, an AFDU aircraft, was the first to be fitted with a Rolls-Royce Merlin engine under the designation Mustang X.

southern England and carrying out coastal patrols on the lookout for enemy fighter-bombers and reconnaissance aircraft. In addition to this task the two squadrons also

year as a Lancaster squadron in No 5 Group Bomber Command.

Three more Mustang I squadrons disbanded before the end of 1943. The first to go, in September, was No 239 Squadron, which had been occupied in TacR operations over France. These operations cost the squadron six Mustangs during this period, the first – AP192 – failing to return after being hit by flak during an airfield reconnaissance to Abbeville on 12 July. Then, on 22 July, the squadron despatched four Mustangs – AM180, AM238, AM239 and AP183 – on TacR missions to the Ypres and Courtrai areas. All four failed to return. The sixth aircraft, AG557, failed to return from an operation on 10 August, being presumed to have flown into the sea off the French coast. Like No 169 Squadron, No 239 moved to Ayr for training as a Mosquito night-fighter unit.

In October 1943 No 613 Squadron exchanged its Mustangs for Mosquito FB.VI fighter-bombers, beginning operations with these aircraft from Lasham in December. Between 14 July 1943 and its disbandment the squadron operated from Snailwell alongside No 309 Squadron, flying many *Lagoon* sorties under the operational control of No 12 Group. Of the five Mustangs lost on operations during this period, three (AG568, AG656 and AM175) were shot down by enemy fighters off the Dutch coast on 18 July, soon after the squadron's arrival

at Snailwell, and two more (AM254 and AP254) suffered the same fate on 27 July.

The other Mustang squadron to change its equipment in 1943 was No 16 at Hartfordbridge, which re-equipped with Spitfire XIs in November to undertake high- and low-level reconnaissance in preparation for the invasion. This squadron, in common with Nos 169 and 170, had been assigned mainly to air defence and had achieved some successes against low-flying Focke-Wulf 190 fighter-bombers attacking coastal towns, although the latter had turned the tables on 30 August when a pair of them damaged AP263 and forced it to ditch in the Channel. It was the squadron's only loss during this period.

In late August and early September 1943, the Tactical Air Force's Mustang squadrons flew intensively in support of Operation *Starkey*, which was designed to test the strength of the *Luftwaffe* in the Channel area. While an amphibious force put to sea and spent several days tacking to and fro in mid-Channel, Mustangs joined other tactical aircraft in strafing attacks on airfields and other targets in France. The Mustangs of Nos 35 and 39 Wings were particularly active in providing photographic reconnaissance, particularly

AM203 was the third Mustang X conversion, flying on 21 January 1943.

of enemy airfields. Unfortunately the *Luftwaffe* failed to react as anticipated, and as a result the exercise was unsuccessful.

The RAF Mustang squadrons that bore the brunt of tactical reconnaissance operations in the latter half of 1943 – Nos 2, 4, 168, 231, 268, 400, 414 and 430 – lost thirty-seven aircraft between them during this period, not all as the result of enemy action. In another tragic case of mis-identification, AP206 of No 414 Squadron was shot down by Spitfires off the Scilly Isles on 17 June 1943, while several other aircraft failed to return as a result of engine failure. This certainly happened to AP241 of No 2 Squadron, which was forced to ditch in the Channel after its Allison engine cut out on 28 August 1943, and the same fate may have overtaken AM109 of the same squadron which went missing on the next day. Other losses thought to have been attributed to engine failure included AG661, AM256 and AP173, all of No 400 Squadron, AM216 of No 168 Squadron and AM167 of No 414 Squadron.

Enemy fighters accounted for at least five Mustangs during the latter half of the year. AL972 of No 2 Squadron was shot down by Fw 190s during a shipping reconnaissance off the Dutch coast on 3 June, and on 25 August another of the squadron's aircraft, AM217, was shot down by Messerschmitt 109s off France. No 4 Squadron also lost AG576 that day, the Mustang falling victim to Fw 190s off Le Havre. No 414 Squadron lost AP172 to the guns of a Fw 190 on 6 June, and another Fw 190 destroyed AP197 of the same squadron off Dunkirk on 8 September. Fighters almost certainly accounted for FD533, FD535 and FD551 of No 268 Squadron, all of which failed to return from tactical reconnaissance sorties to France on 26 September 1943, and AG547 of No 231 Squadron, missing near Cherbourg on 15 November.

Intense flak was an ever-present threat to the low-flying Mustangs. It claimed AM127 and AP238 of No 4 Squadron in an attack on Alkmaar airfield in Holland on 7 July 1943, and the following day the squadron

lost AM127 to flak off Texel during a shipping reconnaissance. Flak also accounted for AM200 of No 430 Squadron over Normandy on 2 June, AP232 of No 268 Squadron, shot down over the Cotentin Peninsula on 30 July, AM111 of No 414 Squadron, shot down while attacking an enemy vessel off the Dutch coast on 5 November, AP261, also of No 414 Squadron, shot down over Alencon on 11 November, and AP169 and FD545 of Nos 2 and 168 Squadrons, the first destroyed near Perry-en-Auge and the other over St Malo, both on 9 November.

Some pilots managed to bring their badly damaged aircraft home. On 16 July the pilot of flak-battered AM187 of No 400 Squadron struggled across the Channel as far as Friston before baling out, and on 8 November AP225 crash-landed at Tangmere after being badly hit. Another 400 Squadron aircraft, AG641, was abandoned ten miles off Dieppe on 22 June following flak damage, the pilot being picked up by RAF Air-Sea Rescue.

The Tactical Air Force Mustangs carried out many 'Ranger' operations in the latter half of 1943, roving over northern France and Belgium in pairs at low altitude seeking targets of opportunity. Sometimes they caught enemy aircraft unawares and achieved notable successes. One such occurred in late June, when two pilots of the Air Fighting Development Unit, Squadron Leader James McLachlan and Flight Lieutenant Geoffrey Page, destroyed four Henschel 126s and two Junkers 88s in the space of ten minutes. The AFDU also pioneered the use of the Mustang in night intruder operations, work for which the aircraft, with its lengthy endurance, was well suited. Only one Mustang was lost during these operations; this was AP224 of No 414 Squadron, which failed to return from a night sortie to Chievres airfield in Belgium on 15 September 1943.

Deliveries of the Merlin-engined Mustang, designated Mustang Mk III in RAF service, began in December 1943, but the first thirty-six aircraft were allocated to the Eighth Air Force to alleviate its shortage of escort fighters. The first RAF squadron to receive the new aircraft was No 65, which was based at Gravesend with Spitfire IXs. A second Gravesend-based unit, No 19 Squadron, also began to replace its Spitfires with Mustang IIIs in February 1944, as did the third squadron of the Gravesend Wing, No 122. In the following month two Polish Spitfire units, Nos 306 'Torunski' and 315 'Deblinski' Squadrons, also equipped with Mustang IIIs at Heston before moving to Coolham in Sussex, where they were joined in April 1944 by No 129 Squadron. The first operational sortie with Mustangs from Coolham was flown on 26 April, when Nos 129 and 315 Squadrons carried out a sweep to Beauvais. The seventh UK-based squadron to receive Mustang IIIs in the first half of 1944 was No 316 'Warszawski', which went to Coltishall, Norfolk, in May 1944 for bomber escort and fighter-bomber duties under the control of No 12 Group. Meanwhile, No 309 Squadron, which had been operating from Snailwell since November 1943, had been experiencing severe problems with the Allison-engined Mustang Is and IAs, and in February 1944 it was sent to Drem in Scotland for air defence duties with Hurricane IICs and IVs. A month earlier No 231 Squadron, after operating its Mustang Is for less than a year, had disbanded at Redhill; it was later reformed in Canada as a long-range ferry and communications unit.

No 4 Squadron also relinquished its Mustangs in January 1944, re-equipping with Spitfire XIs and Mosquito XVIs for photo-reconnaissance duties. Operating out of Gatwick, it formed No 35 Tactical Reconnaissance Wing alongside the Mustang-equipped Nos 2 and 268 Squadrons. In February No 400 RCAF Squadron also converted to a mixture of Spitfires and Mosquitoes for similar duties, forming No 39 Tactical Reconnaissance Wing at Odiham together with Nos 414 and 430 Squadrons RCAF and No 168 Squadron, all still flying Mustangs. The third squadron to lose its Mustangs in February 1944 was No 516 in

Mustang III of No 309 (Polish) Squadron.

Scotland, which continued to operate Blenheim IVs and Hurricanes until the end of the year, when there was no longer a requirement for it and it was disbanded.

Then, in March 1944, No 26 Squadron, which had been engaged in Army co-operation duties at Ayr and various other Scottish locations, staged south through Hutton Cranswick in Yorkshire to Lee-on-Solent where, newly equipped with Spitfire Vs, it began training in naval gunnery spotting. No 26 Squadron, the pioneer Mustang unit, would not operate the American-built fighters again until January 1945. In May No 63 Squadron also arrived at Lee-on-Solent from Scotland, having re-equipped with Spitfire Vs. The two former Mustang squadrons formed the Air Spotting Pool together with four Fleet Air Arm squadrons and a flight of Typhoons, the joint task being the direction of naval gunfire on and after D-Day.

The activities of the Tactical Reconnaissance Wings in the early part of 1944 were to prove of inestimable value to the eventual success of the invasion. From February onwards, for example, aircraft of No 35 Recce Wing, acting on intelligence reports, photographed the sea bed off the Normandy coast, and it was quickly established that the Germans had begun laying obstacles. From then on, regular reconnaissance of the beaches were undertaken to monitor enemy progress, the Mustangs taking some remarkable low-level oblique photographs when high-level photography was not possible because of adverse weather conditions.

On another occasion, an experiment was carried out to see if rocket projectiles would be effective in destroying radar installations, and an enemy radar site in Holland was chosen as the target for rocket-firing Typhoons. Post-strike photographs by Mosquitos and Spitfires failed to show damage, so the Central Interpretation Unit briefed the Mustang pilots of No 168 Squadron, 39 Wing, to take very close oblique photographs. The sortie, flown on 16 May 1944, showed that the attack had

been completely successful, and from then on rocket attacks against enemy coastal radar installations became routine in the weeks prior to D-Day.

A great deal of low-level photo-reconnaissance work was also carried out during the pre-invasion period by the F-6 Mustangs of the USAAF's 67th Photographic Reconnaissance Group, which had been assigned to the Ninth Air Force since October 1943 and whose 12th and 107th Squadrons became operational at Middle Wallop in January 1944. Between 23 February and 20 March they carried out oblique photography of 160 miles of the French coastline, the task being taken over by the 15th and 109th Squadrons in April. The low-level photographs enabled the invasion planners to study the enemy's Atlantic Wall defences in minute detail, to brief assault troops, study local topography and assess activity in marshalling yards and on airfields.

Meanwhile, other RAF Mustang squadrons had been engaged in bomber escort and extensive attacks on airfields and other targets in enemy territory, the three squadrons (Nos 19, 65 and 122) of No 122 Wing, 83 Group, at Funtington in Sussex being very active in this respect. On 17 May, five Mustang IIIs of No 65 Squadron and two from No 122 refuelled at Coltishall and then flew 400 nautical miles to Aalborg in Denmark, where they discovered a crowded airfield and made a highly successful strafing attack, claiming the destruction of five Junkers Ju 88s, two Heinkel He 177s, a Messerschmitt Bf 109, and four Junkers W.34s. In addition, the pilots claimed two Arado Ar 196 floatplanes damaged at their moorings in the adjacent seaplane base. The two squadrons lost two Mustangs in the operation, but one pilot, Sgt R.T. Williams, successfully evaded capture and got away to Sweden, from where he was eventually repatriated. Another attack on Aalborg was carried out by No 19 Squadron on 21 May, the squadron losing two Mustangs, FB158 and FX999, both falling prey to fighters.

The Mustangs of No 122 Wing also undertook several escort missions in the spring of 1944, accompanying Eighth Air Force B-17s to various targets in Germany, Nos 19 and 122 Squadrons losing nine aircraft in two months of these operations. The first such loss was FZ188 of No 19 Squadron, which went missing in cloud on a B-17 escort to Leipzig on 4 March, and on 9 March the squadron lost FZ178, which was hit by flak and abandoned over Celle, and FX973, which crashed in the Thames Estuary through unknown causes as it returned from the raid. The other losses were all sustained by No 122 Squadron. FZ102 was hit by flak and crashed in Holland on 8 April; FZ108, also hit by flak, was abandoned over the Dutch coast two days later, and the same fate overtook FZ131 near Metz on the last day of the month. On 7 May FX971 was shot down by flak near Osnabruck, on 18 May FZ164 was accounted for by flak near Tours, and on the following day FZ168 was abandoned after a collision in cloud during a bomber escort mission. The main reason for the losses to flak was that the RAF Mustangs were briefed to operate at medium level on the lookout for enemy fighters climbing away from their airfields, the Eighth Air Force's Mustangs operating much higher up. Eleven enemy fighters were claimed by No 122 Wing in April and May.

The Mustangs of No 133 Wing, 84 Group (Nos 129, 306 and 305 Squadrons) at Coloham, Sussex, also carried out some bomber escort missions, but their primary concern was the precision bombing of marshalling yards and other objectives in France and the Low Countries. These attacks, in which all Allied tactical aircraft except those earmarked for bomber escort missions took part – and even those had *carte blanche* to attack rolling stock and other targets of opportunity if they had ammunition left on the homeward run – were made in conjunction with a policy (formulated by Air Chief Marshal Sir Arthur Tedder, the Allied Deputy Supreme Commander) of sustained air attacks on

312102, originally a P-51B-1-NA, was an early conversion to P-51D configuration. The dorsal fairing has not yet been added.

enemy railways, rolling stock, marshalling yards, repair and maintenance facilities, roads and bridges – in other words, anything that would impede the transfer of German reinforcements to the battlefront. The plan was bitterly opposed by General Carl Spaatz, commanding the US Strategic Air Force, who wanted the main air offensive to be concentrated against oil targets. Nevertheless, Tedder had his way, and in the two months prior to 6 June 1944 Allied bombers and fighter-bombers dropped 66,517 tons of bombs on eighty selected targets, mostly involving railways.

It was not until the Allies set foot on the continent and began to push deeper inland that the full extent of the havoc wrought by air attacks on enemy communications was appreciated. By D-Day, the enemy transport system in western Europe was on the verge of collapse, a state of affairs brought about mainly by heavy attacks on marshalling yards and repair centres.

Meanwhile, both the British and Americans had been seeking to remedy one of the Mustang's most serious short-comings, which was poor visibility from the cockpit. The British answer was to adopt a bulged sliding cockpit canopy designed by Malcolm Aircraft Ltd of Slough, Buckinghamshire, who were producing canopies for high-altitude aircraft such as the Spitfire Mk VI; this was retrofitted to the RAF's Mustang IIIs and also to some of the USAAF's P-51Cs. The real solution to the problem, however, was found by North American, who tested two P-51Bs (42-106539 and 42-106540) with a 360-degree vision 'teardrop' one-piece sliding canopy and cut-down rear fuselage. These conversions, designated XP-51D-NA, also had six .50 calibre Browning air-cooled machine guns with 1,880 rounds in a strengthened wing. The aircraft were also later fitted with a dorsal fin to compensate for the loss of keel surface after the removal of the upper rear fuselage. Other refinements in the course of production included the addition of two sets of stub rocket launchers under each wing to carry five-inch rockets.

The first production P-51Ds to arrive in the United Kingdom in the late spring of 1944 were assigned to group, squadron and flight commanders, who needed better visibility to exercise tactical control of their formations. The P-51D was marginally slower than the P-51B/C, but its six-gun armament was better suited to strafing attacks. The latter, particularly against airfields, were now becoming very costly affairs as the Germans strengthened their airfield defences. While the Mustangs of the RAF's 2nd Tactical Air Force and the P-51s of the USAAF's IX Tactical Air Command concentrated on airfield targets in France in the weeks immediately before D-Day, particularly those within a 150-mile radius of Caen, the Eighth Air Force's P-51s ranged farther afield, their long bomber escort missions alternating with attacks on airfields in Germany and the Low Countries.

One of the most successful missions flown by VIII Fighter Command during this period occurred on 21 May 1944, when 617 Mustangs, Thunderbolts and Lightnings claimed the destruction of eighty-three enemy aircraft on the ground, with a further sixty-seven destroyed or damaged. In addition, the fighter-bombers positively destroyed ninety-one locomotives and attacked 134 other targets, including railway stations and river traffic.

The first week in June came as something of an anti-climax, with operations being hampered by bad weather. But by Saturday, 3 June, it became apparent that the invasion was imminent, and the next day the tactical aircraft of the Allied Expeditionary Air Force were fuelled, armed and painted with black-and-white recognition stripes, ready for the great event, and masked under camouflage netting to shield them from enemy reconnaissance aircraft. The latter precaution, though appropriate, was not really necessary. For some weeks now, thanks to the effective air defence patrols flown by Mustangs and other types, no German reconnaissance aircraft had succeeded in penetrating the south coast defences.

Chapter 5
D-Day and After: 2TAF, RAF Fighter
Command and Ninth Air Force

ALL THE Mustang-equipped squadrons of the RAF took part in the Allied invasion of Normandy with the exception of No 316, which remained in East Anglia for 2 Group bomber escort duties against targets in Holland, air defence and shipping reconnaissance. The seven P-51 groups of the US Eighth Air Force and the two of Ninth Air Force also participated throughout D-Day, flying relays of defensive patrols over the invasion fleet and attacking targets inland as required, although the latter task in these early stages was undertaken mainly by the twin-engined tactical bombers of 2nd TAF and IX Tactical Air Command.

Immediate top cover over the invasion forces was undertaken by the Eighth Air

Force's P-38 Lightning groups, the twin-tailed P-38 being easily identifiable to the naval gunners who had an understandable tendency to shoot at any aircraft that came too close. The sortie rate varied depending on the task allotted to individual groups; the 352nd FG, for example, put up nine patrols, the 357th eight and the 355th six, the latter group claiming fifteen out of a total of twenty-six enemy aircraft destroyed by the USAAF on this day. The 4th FG from Debden, which also put up six patrols, had a bad day, being bounced by fifteen Fw 190s and Bf 109s during an evening patrol in the Rouen sector and losing seven P-51s. All four aircraft in the 355th Squadron's Blue Section were quickly shot down, followed by one from the 334th and 335th FS. The

Mustang pair: a fine air-to-air study of P-51Ds on patrol.

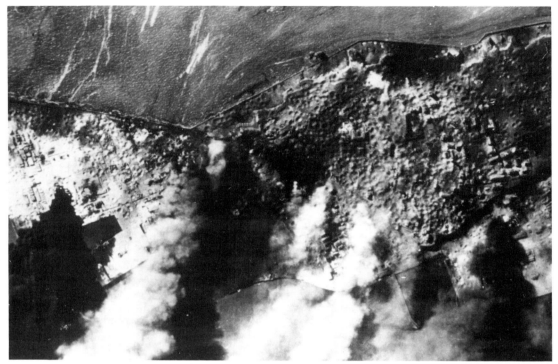

D-Day. Air reconnaissance photograph reveals the heavily-cratered Normandy beach-head shrouded in smoke.

seventh loss was a pilot from the 339th FS, who had come over to Debden in order to fly with his old group on D-Day. On the credit side, the group could claim only four Fw 190s destroyed.

The RAF lost three Mustangs, all Mk Is, during the operations of 6 June 1944. One of these, AM225 of No 168 Squadron, exploded in mid-air over the Channel and was thought to have been hit by a shell from one of the bombarding warships, while AG465 of No 430 Squadron was shot down by Fw 190s near Évreux during a TacR sortie. The third Mustang, FD495 of No 268 Squadron, failed to return, its fate unknown.

On 7 June, with the spearhead divisions safely ashore and reinforcements pouring into the newly-won beachheads, the weight of tactical air power was thrown against the enemy armoured divisions that were heading for the Normandy coast. On this day the six Mustang Mk III Squadrons of No 84 Group, which had been held in reserve on D-Day itself, were thrown into the battle in their role of ground support, joining eighteen squadrons of Typhoons, and the Germans soon learned to their cost the folly of moving large formations in daylight in the face of overwhelming tactical air superiority.

In this context, the experience of the *Panzer Lehr* Division was typical. One of the best divisions in the German Army, led by the able Lieutenant-General Fritz Bayerlein, who had been Rommel's *Afrika Korps* chief of staff, *Panzer Lehr* was savaged during its move on 7 June from the Chartres area to the Seulles Valley. Bayerlein, the desert veteran, knew all about the perils of moving armour across open country by day, but his objections were overruled by the Seventh Army commander, General Dollman, and as a result *Panzer Lehr* suffered appalling losses by the time its nightmare journey ended. Early in the morning of 7 June, the division was attacked by Typhoons and Mustangs, which destroyed 130 trucks and fuel tankers, five tanks and eighty-four self-propelled guns, half-tracks and other vehicles. Seven Mustangs were shot down by flak during the attacks, No 306 Squadron losing four and Nos 19, 122 and 129 one each, but tactical air power had robbed the Seventh Army of its only fighting-efficient, full-strength armoured division in Normandy.

Only one RAF Mustang was lost on the following day, when AM128 of No 168 Squadron failed to return from a tactical reconnaissance. Despite the engine troubles that continued to plague the Mk I, one Canadian pilot of No 39 Reconnaissance Wing later wrote: 'We were happy with our reliable fighters . . . the Mustang had satisfied everyone with its ruggedness, reliability and comforting high speed. The only disappointments were its lack of dogfighting manoeuvrability and its inability to operate effectively at high altitudes. It was a big, impressive fighter, a much larger machine than the Spitfires of the day. Painted in the dark greens of RAF camouflage and polished with loving care, the Mustang I was a sleek, beautiful aeroplane.'

The same pilot also described a typical reconnaissance by a section of three Mustangs. 'We flew . . . with about two hundred yards between the lead aircraft and the two of us with him, one on each side. Each of us had begun flying as if we were on a rollercoaster swinging from side to side, then up and down, changing altitude in a range of some five hundred feet. We had learned that without this constant change of line and altitude, the incredible German 88 anti-aircraft gun would be putting their vicious black shells either into our aircraft or close enough that we could hear them explode. The rule was: "If they're close enough that you can hear

A typical advanced landing ground in Normandy. The taxying aircraft is a Tempest V of No 122 Wing.

Allied air superiority kept the *Luftwaffe* at bay. Here, a Focke-Wulf 190 falls victim to a Mustang.

them explode you're in real trouble." Even so, as we crossed the enemy lines either going out or coming back in that dense, heavily defended sector, the rollercoaster movement was no guarantee against being hit.'

And there was no doubt that the enemy flak *was* murderous. On 10 June it accounted for six out of seven RAF Mustangs lost on operations that day, the seventh aircraft, FX884 of No 65 Squadron, being shot down by Messerschmitt 109s. No 65 Squadron lost a second aircraft; No 315 Squadron also lost two, while Nos 129, 306 and 414 Squadrons lost one each. Both the 315 Squadron pilots were able to bale out over friendly territory. On the next day No 65 squadron lost a second aircraft, FB102, to 109s; it was the RAF's only Mustang loss on 11 June. The Messerschmitts also claimed Mustang IA FD552 of No 268 Squadron near Louviers

on 14 June, but these were isolated instances; Allied air superiority kept the *Luftwaffe* at bay, and it was the flak that caused most of the losses.

Between 6 June 1944 and the end of the month the RAF Mustang squadrons operating over Normandy lost sixty-three aircraft, nearly twice as many as the total lost in the first half of the year. The hardest hit was No 306 (Polish) Squadron, which lost ten, followed by No 65 Squadron with eight, No 414 RCAF Squadron with seven, Nos 119 and 168 Squadrons with six each, Nos 2, 19, 268 and 315 Squadrons with five each, No 430 with four and No 122 with two. The *Luftwaffe* fighters were particularly active on 24 June, claiming six Mustangs. The main reason for the upsurge in enemy fighter intercepts was that, from 20 June, the heavy bombers of VIII Bomber Command and the RAF joined the tactical air forces in mounting a series of attacks against selected target areas in support of the Allied attempt to break out of the Normandy beachhead.

During the last week of June the 2 TAF Mustang squadrons began moving to advanced landing grounds in Normandy in support of 21st Army Group's breakout. The first to cross the Channel were Nos 19, 65 and 122 Squadrons of No 122 Wing, which moved to B.7 Martagny on 25 June, and on 29 June No 168 Squadron went to B.8 Sommervieu. Plans were in fact made to send the whole of 2 TAF's Mustang strength to France in support of 21st Army Group, but these were frustrated by a new and alarming development.

On the night of 12/13 June 1944, while bombing operations in support of the Allied offensive in Normandy were still in full swing, the first V-1 flying bomb was launched against London from a site in the Pas de Calais. The launch sites had been frequently attacked by the RAF and USAAF since their existence was first established late in 1943 – in fact, the PR Mustangs of Nos 35 and 39 Wings had played a leading part in amassing vital low-level oblique photographic coverage – but they were extremely well camouflaged and well defended, and although the attacks had slowed down the construction programme they had not succeeded in halting it.

For the fighter pilots engaged in air defence against the V-1, the main problem was one of rapid response and accurate control. Their small margin of speed over the flying bombs, coupled with the short time available to make an interception, demanded that they should be quickly and accurately directed onto the V-1's course before the missile reached the gun and balloon belts. There was consequently a major problem of warning and control to be solved, because the network of radar stations, Observer Corps posts, telecommunications and Fighter Command operations rooms, which had evolved so successfully earlier in the war to counter attacks by piloted aircraft, suddenly became outmoded in the face of this new threat. The same was true of the defence system as a whole; it was not just a matter of improving the efficiency of the guns, searchlights, balloons and fighters as separate weapons, but of co-ordinating their activities. This co-ordination was vital, especially between guns and fighters.

As the Operations Room at No 11 Group HQ was fully occupied in controlling fighter activities over the Normandy beach-head in June 1944, all anti-V-1 ('Diver') defences were controlled by the Operations room of the Biggin Hill Sector. This was linked with the operations rooms of Anti-Aircraft Command in the 'Diver' area, and all information from the radar stations and the Royal Observer Corps was fed into it. However, the control that was exercised by Biggin Hill was general rather than specific, and much different from the procedure that had normally been employed in the defence against piloted aircraft, where the direction of intercepting fighters was the responsibility of the sector operations room. Instead, executive control of the patrolling fighters was vested in the same agencies that detected and plotted the flying bombs; the radar stations and the Observer Corps centres at Horsham and Maidstone were used as fighter direction stations. Similarly, Anti-Aircraft Command found it impracticable to control the firing of individual batteries from gun operations rooms, and so batteries were allowed to fire independently except when the gun operations room ordered fire to cease – in order to safeguard friendly aircraft, for example.

The system worked in that it reduced the time between detection and interception, but it had to be supplemented by a set of standing orders designed to avoid mutual interference between guns, fighters and balloons. Weather, too, was a prime consideration. As early as 16 June Air Marshal Sir Roderic Hill, commanding the Air Defence of Great Britain (himself an accomplished pilot who took part in sixty-two 'Diver' patrols, flying each type of defensive fighter in turn), decided that fighters would patrol over the Channel and

The V-1 presented a small and difficult target, as this photograph shows. The V-1 is at top right, being pursued by a Tempest.

'Flabby', 'Spouse' and 'Fickle'. In the case of 'Flabby', there was to be a total prohibition of gunfire when the weather was suitable for fighters; 'Spouse', which came into force when the weather was unsuitable for fighters, allowed complete freedom to the guns; and 'Fickle', in average weather conditions, permitted the guns to fire in the 'Diver' belt up to 8,000 feet. Fighters were prohibited from entering the belt except when making a visual interception; outside the 'Diver' belt fighters were given complete freedom of action, and light anti-aircraft guns were allowed to fire by day against visual targets if no fighters were present.

However, although these rules went some way towards tackling the problem, they did not solve it. Fighter pilots frequently reported that they had been engaged by the guns, and the gunners no less frequently reported that their shooting had been hindered by the fighters. It was not until the whole scheme of defence was radically altered in the middle of July that the difficulties began to be overcome.

Of the eleven RAF fighter squadrons assigned to 'Diver' operations, four were equipped with Mustang Mk IIIs. These were Nos 129, 306, 315 and 316 Squadrons. Early in July the first three were deployed in Brenzett, in Kent, while No 316 went to Friston in Sussex to operate alongside the Spitfire XIIs and XIVs of Nos 41 and 610 Squadrons.

The Mustang, with its high diving speed and its inherent stability as a gun platform, proved well suited to the task in hand, but the pilots were soon made aware of the problems associated with intercepting the flying bombs. The principal problem was one of obtaining accurate information on the course of the V-1 in order to transmit it rapidly from the sources on the ground via the fighter controller to the patrolling pilot, but it did not end there. The pilot, having been told where to look for his target, had to find it. By day this was not easy, for the flying bombs were extremely difficult to spot; apart from the fact that they presented

the strip of land between the coast and the southern limit of the gun belt. They were permitted to pass over the gun belt only when in pursuit of a flying bomb, in which case the guns were not to open fire. On 19 June it was decided that on days of very good visibility only the fighters would operate, and on bad days only the guns. On moderate days both guns and fighters would operate, each in their own areas.

These principles were expanded on 26 June under the curious code-names of a diminutive target, with their sixteen-foot wingspan and twenty-foot length, their upper surfaces were camouflaged – usually in two shades of brown – which, at their lower operating altitude, rendered them almost invisible against the landscape to a pilot patrolling higher up. The trick was to locate them over the sea and then try to keep them in sight. Experience soon showed that the V-1s could be most readily picked up in twilight, when the flame from their pulse-jet engines showed up clearly, and 'Flabby' – complete freedom of action for the fighters – was frequently instituted at dawn and dusk for this reason.

By the end of June two methods of controlling the ADGB fighters had been evolved, one for controlling the fighters over the Channel and the other for the direction of fighters patrolling over land. The first of these – the close control method – involved the direction of individual fighters by controllers located at radar stations on the coast. Approaching flying bombs were plotted in the control room of the radar station from which the controller, who was in R/T communication with the patrolling fighter, would issue detailed instructions on the bomb's course so as to bring the pilot into a position to intercept. The factor limiting the extent to which this method could be used was the number of control points available; by the middle of July only four radar stations were engaged in close control.

The main practical difficulty was that existing types of radar station could not, for technical reasons, provide sufficient early warning of an approaching bomb. The best of the stations rarely detected the bombs at ranges of more than 50 miles, which meant that the fighter had, even in theory, no more than six minutes in which to intercept the bomb before it reached the coast. In practice it had less; first because there was a substantial time lag between the initial detection of a bomb and the transmission of interception data from the fighter controller to the pilot, and secondly because patrols could not be carried out at the limit of the radar detection range because of the risk of being surprised by enemy fighters. In the Strait of Dover the ADGB fighters had three minutes at the outside in which to intercept a V-1 before the missile reached the Kent coast.

Despite the shortcomings, ADGB persevered with the close control method, because successful interceptions resulted in the bombs falling harmlessly into the sea. Over land, where there were no low-looking radar facilities, the running commentary method was used. The controllers using this technique were located at three radar stations – Beachy Head, Hythe and Sandwich – and two Observer Corps centres, Horsham and Maidstone. In the running commentary method, the position and course of the flying bomb were passed on the same R/T frequency to all patrolling fighters, whose pilots then worked out their own course to intercept the target. This method was also

Shooting down V-1s was a risky business. Here, a flying bomb explodes in mid-air.

used for fighters patrolling seaward, but it worked best over land where shellbursts, rockets from Observer Corps posts, searchlight beams and landmarks all helped the pilots to make speedy interceptions. The chief drawback was that more than one fighter often went after the same flying bomb, a waste of effort which meant that some V-1s slipped through unmolested.

Engaging and destroying the V-1s also brought its own problems. Chasing a flying bomb from astern meant a long and probably fruitless pursuit unless the fighter pilot had the advantage of height at the moment of sighting. The best method of closing to attack, therefore, was to fly on the same – or nearly the same – course as that of an approaching flying bomb so that it came to the fighter, rather than the other way round.

Because of the high speed at which interceptions took place there were only brief opportunities for deflection shooting, and the vast majority of V-1s accounted for by ADGB fighters were destroyed from astern. Here, too, there were problems; even if the fighter pilot succeeded in closing to within firing range, the flying bomb's slipstream and jet efflux made it difficult to hold a steady aim, so that short bursts of fire and frequent aiming corrections were necessary. The shorter the range, the more effective the fire, although this general rule applied down to a range of not less than 200 yards; any closer and the fighter risked being destroyed by the blast of the V-1's warhead. One No 316 Squadron pilot found this to his cost on 12 July, when he was forced to abandon his Mustang after it was struck by flying debris. To cap it all, pilots soon found that the flying bombs were robust enough to absorb a great deal of punishment before exploding or being brought down.

Although the three Hawker Tempest Mk V squadrons of No 150 Wing, with their superior speed and cannon armament, were a long way out in front in terms of missiles destroyed during the V-1 battle – Nos 3 and 486 (RNZAF) Squadrons destroying nearly

500 between them – the Mustang squadrons gave a creditable account of themselves. During the hectic two-month period at the height of the battle the squadrons of No 133 Wing at Brenzett destroyed 179 flying bombs, while No 316 Squadron at Friston destroyed seventy-five. No 133 Wing lost only one Mustang during these operations; on 29 July, FB241 of No 306 Squadron was tragically shot down by anti-aircraft fire as it was chasing a V-1 near Hastings.

The Mustangs of the 354th Fighter Group, whose airfield at Lashenden lay directly under the V-1s' flight path, also intercepted and destroyed a number of flying bombs before the Group moved across the Channel to A.2 (Criqueville) on 23 June. Lieutenant J. Powers of the 355th Fighter Squadron was the Group's most successful pilot, destroying two V-1s in one sortie and sharing in the destruction of a third.

Throughout the V-1 campaign, excellent photographic reconnaissance support was given by the Mustangs of No 39 Wing and also by No 106 Group, which operated a mixture of PR Spitfires and Mosquitos from RAF Benson in Oxfordshire. With target material obtained by photographic reconnaissance, the Allied bombing attacks against the V-1 firing sites were so successful that never more than about one-third of the total were capable of launching flying bombs at any one time. As part of the plan of attack it was decided to launch heavy raids on the supply sites, and also on the areas where the flying bombs and their fuel might be manufactured, when industrial targets in Germany were thought to be connected with this production.

It was soon ascertained from ground information, and confirmed by photographic reconnaissance, that a number of storage depots were being prepared in the vicinity of the flying-bomb sites and that these were of more importance as targets than the supply sites. In an effort to escape notice and to nullify the effects of bombing, most of these were situated underground, in caves, quarry sides and similar positions, and vertical photography was of little use in obtaining the details necessary for successful bombing. Remarkable results were obtained by low-flying Mosquitos with a single forward-facing oblique camera fitted in the nose, the aircraft diving straight onto the target, but this method subjected the aircraft to a great deal of danger from flak as it flew straight on to its target at a height of about 200 feet, and No 106 Group did its best to discourage such sorties unless they were absolutely essential.

Three Mustang Mk IAs with short focal length cameras were also lent by the Allied Expeditionary Air Force to No 541 Squadron for this special task, and their pilots were able to take photographs below cloud level at 3,000 to 5,000 feet. They could obtain obliques without flying straight onto the target, although the results were not quite as good as those obtained with the forward-facing camera. On 15 August 1944, two Mustangs flown by South African Air Force pilots, Captain Williams and Lieutenant Godden, took amazing low-level obliques of the entrance to mushroom caves

at Leu d'Esserent which had been enlarged, fitted with steel and concrete doors and used as a flying bomb storage depot. These sorties supplied the technical data necessary for the successful bombing of the storage site, which blocked the entrance by causing heavy subsidence of the overhanging soil.

On 28 June 1944 the TacR Mustangs of No 39 Wing began their move from Odiham to B.8, an advanced landing ground near Sommervieu, Bayeux. The first to leave was No 430 Squadron, followed by No 168 Squadron and the Spitfire element of No 400 Squadron, the Mosquitos remaining at Odiham until 14 August, when they too left for Normandy with the Mustangs of No 414 Squadron. No 39 Wing was replaced at Odiham by No 35 Wing, which began its move on 27 June, although the Mustangs of Nos 2 and 268 Squadrons soon departed for B.10 Plumetot, to be followed in mid-August by the PR Spitfires of No 4 Squadron. By this time No 268 Squadron was also operating Typhoons in the tactical reconnaissance role alongside its Mustangs.

Mustangs of the 406th Fighter Group on patrol.

Attacks on rolling stock paralysed German attempts to reinforce Normandy.

Of the RAF Mustang squadrons that moved to France in support of 21st Army Group's drive through the Low Countries in the autumn of 1944, all were to retain the North American fighter as their primary equipment with the exception of No 168, which began converting to Typhoons in September.

On 7 August 1944, RAF Mustangs joined Typhoons in the smashing of a German armoured counter-attack in the Mortain sector. Ten days later, the remnants of sixteen German divisions, including nine Panzer divisions, were trapped in a twenty-five-mile-wide corridor near Falaise and systematically destroyed by concentrated air attacks. On average, the Typhoon, Mustang and Spitfire pilots of 2nd TAF flew 1,200 sorties a day; the *Luftwaffe*'s available fighter squadrons, desperately trying to stem the slaughter, were decimated.

After Falaise the breakout was rapid. While the Americans and Fighting French pushed on to liberate Paris and its environs, the British Second Army crossed the Seine and crossed the Belgian frontier. The difficulty for the squadrons of 2nd TAF now was in keeping up with the speed of the advance; the repair of captured airfields assumed top priority, for there was no longer even time to construct temporary strips.

In September 1944, a policy change resulted in the three Mustang squadrons of No 122 Wing (Nos 19, 65 and 122) being moved back to the United Kingdom. RAF Bomber Command was now carrying out increasing numbers of daylight operations, and every available Mustang was needed for long-range escort duties. In many quarters, the prospect of using the RAF's heavy bomber for daylight attacks on a large scale was viewed with serious misgivings, and there was no denying that the small number of daylight attacks carried out by Bomber Command in 1942 had been accompanied by heavy losses. By the summer of 1944, however, the situation was different. Although the Lancasters and Halifaxes could not operate satisfactorily in formation at altitudes greater than 19,000 feet , where they were vulnerable to heavy flak, they now had the benefit of long-range fighter escort, something that had been lacking in 1942-3. With strong fighter escort, the Air Staff felt, there was no reason why the heavy bombers should not penetrate to targets deep inside occupied territory and even in western Germany, provided such targets were not too heavily defended and the attacking forces were carefully routed.

The theory was put to the test in June 1944, when a total of 2,716 sorties were sent out in daylight to targets in Occupied Europe. The majority of these were flown by Lancasters and Halifaxes, and the loss rate was only 0.4 per cent – an extremely low casualty figure attributable in the main to the lack of day fighter opposition. In July the number of sorties despatched was 6,847, and once again the loss rate was only 0.4 per cent. All these sorties, however, had been relatively short-range operations against poorly-defended targets, and full fighter cover had been provided by the Spitfires of No 11 Group.

It was not until the end of August 1944 that RAF heavy bombers penetrated into Germany with fighter escort. On the 27th, 216 Halifaxes of No 4 Group, together with twenty-seven Mosquitos and Lancasters of the Pathfinder Force, were despatched to attack the oil plant at Homburg, in the Ruhr. The bombers were accompanied on the outward trip by nine squadrons of Spitfires; seven more Spitfire squadrons arrived over the target at the same time as the bombers, providing a strengthened escort on the homeward run. Only one enemy fighter, a Messerschmitt 110, was sighted, and this made no attempt to attack. Despite very heavy anti-aircraft fire over Homburg all the attacking force returned to base. The target itself was severely damaged.

Encouraged, Bomber Command authorised another major daylight operation against Germany. In the early evening of 6 September, 181 Lancasters and Halifaxes of No 6 Group and the PFF were

Escorted by Mustangs, RAF Lancasters and Halifaxes mounted daylight attacks on targets in Occupied Europe. Photograph shows a Halifax over Caen.

Mustang I of No 26 Squadron, 1945. The squadron re-equipped with the Mustangs in January that year.

In the United Kingdom, the long-range Mustang force was further strengthened, in January 1945, by the conversion of No 126 Squadron to Mustang IIIs at Bentwaters in Suffolk. In that same month No 26 Squadron, the original RAF Mustang unit, re-equipped with Mustang Mk Is and moved to North Weald to undertake tactical reconnaissance sorties over the Netherlands. It also provided gunnery

spotting facilities for French warships bombarding German pockets of resistance in the Bordeaux area. The last RAF squadron in the UK to receive Mustangs during the war was No 611, which began to re-equip in January at Hawkinge for bomber escort duties; this was the first RAF squadron in the UK to receive the Mustang Mk IV, as the P-51D and K variants were designated in RAF service. Many RAF P-51Ks, in fact, were designated Mustang Mk IVA.

The P-51K was identical to the P51-D except that it featured an Aeroproducts propeller instead of the Hamilton Standard unit, and some had underwing rails for four 5-in HVAR rockets.

While the P-51D was the standard equipment of the USAAF VIII Fighter Command during the Normandy offensive, the Ninth Air Force (XIX Tactical Air Command) Mustang groups continued to use the P-51B/C. The 354th Fighter Group took its aircraft to A.2 Criqueville, ten miles behind the front line, during the last week

P-51D of the 33rd FG, Raydon, 1944.

P-51D of the 505th FS, 339th FG, displays six 'kills'.

of June 1944, and flew many ground support and counter-air operations from this location before moving to A.31 Gael, France, on 13 August. On the 25th of that month the 354th carried out six fighter sweeps, which earned it its second Distinguished Unit Citation (the first having been awarded for its pioneer long-range escort fighter work), and in the course of that day its pilots destroyed fifty-one enemy aircraft in the air and on the ground, a new record for the Americans in Europe. On 17 September the group moved to A.66 Orconte, but almost had to cease operations in November when the River Marne burst its banks and flooded the base. Then came a bitter blow: the 354th FG was ordered to give up its P-51B/Cs and re-equip with P-47 Thunderbolts, which were now standard equipment with the XIX Tactical Air Command fighter groups. Although the group did much excellent work with the P-47, its personnel were dissatisfied with the change and, after much lobbying in official circles, they were once again authorized to re-equip with the Mustang. With new P-51Ds, the 354th supported the Rhine crossings in March 1945 and, on 8 April, moved to Ober Olm in Germany. On the 15th of that month the group carried out intensive strafing on enemy airfields in

Czechoslovakia and achieved a high score, the 355th Fighter Squadron alone claiming twenty-nine enemy aircraft destroyed on the ground and thirty damaged.

On 30 April 1945 the group moved to R.45 Ansbach, from where it flew its last operational sorties of World War Two. In seventeen months of combat the 354th FG had flown 1,384 missions – 18,334 individual aircraft sorties – claiming 956 enemy aircraft destroyed, thirty-two probably destroyed and 428 damaged against the loss of 178 pilots on operations. Of these victories, 701 were in air-to-air combat, giving the 354th Fighter Group more kills than any other USAAF group in World War Two.

After the war, the 354th FG became part of the Army of Occupation, moving to Herzogenaurach on 18 May 1945. On 15 February 1946 it was transferred, without personnel, to Bolling Field, Washington DC, where it was de-activated on 31 March 1946.

The 354th's sister Mustang group in XIX Tactical Air Command, the 363rd Fighter Group, was re-designated the 363rd Tactical Reconnaissance Group in September 1944, following operations in Normandy, having moved from Staplehurst in Kent to A.15 Maupertuis. Equipped with F-5 and F-6 aircraft, it supported the US Ninth Army's

P-51Ds of the 375th FS, 361st FG, on an escort mission to Germany, late 1944.

drive across the Rhine and remained in Germany until December 1945, when it returned to the United States to be de-activated.

The 10th Tactical Reconnaissance group, assigned to IX Tactical Air Command, was equipped with F-5 Lightnings until June 1944, when it exchanged its 30th and 33rd Squadrons with the 67th Tactical Reconnaissance Group's 12th and 15th Squadrons, which were equipped with F-6B and F-6C Mustangs. Wing guns were retained and the pilots frequently engaged enemy aircraft; one of them, Captain Clyde

Photograph taken by an escorting Mustang shows B-24s on the way to their target.

East of the 15th TR Squadron, was credited with fifteen victories by the end of hostilities, a record for a reconnaissance pilot.

In July 1944 the 10th TRG began moving from Chalgrove to advanced landing grounds near Le Molay and lent TacR support to the US Third Army in the St Lo offensive early in August. The group arrived at Conflans/Doncourt at the end of November and supported US forces during the Ardennes offensive. In January 1945 the 10th TRG flew 732 sorties, claiming the destruction of one enemy aircraft but losing four of its own. April 1945 was the group's busiest month of the war, with 2,179 sorties.

In fourteen months of operations the 10th TRG claimed the destruction of ninety-four enemy aircraft for the loss of fifty-seven F-5s and F-6s, mainly to ground fire. On 8 May 1945, the day on which hostilities in Europe officially ceased, two F-6 Mustangs of the 12th TRS were patrolling the Danube when they were attacked by five Fw 190s. The Mustang pilots evaded the enemy's single pass and went after the 190s in a high-speed climbing turn. The element leader, Lt Robert C. Little, shot down the trailing Focke-Wulf; it was claimed to be the last enemy aircraft destroyed in combat over Europe. (In fact it may not have been; on 9 May, 1945, Guards Major Victor Golubev of the Soviet Air Force shot down a Messerschmitt 109 over Prague, where German forces were still resisting). The 10th TRG remained at Furth, Germany, until June 1947, when it transferred to the United States and re-equipped with RF-51s. It was de-activated on 1 April 1949, but was subsequently re-activated with jet equipment and returned to Germany in 1952.

Before the end of the war in Europe another USAAF fighter group had been assigned to the Ninth Air Force, also in IX Tactical Air Command. This was the 370th FG of the 70th Fighter Wing, which began converting from P-47s to P-51s in February/March 1945, in time to support the Allied crossing of the Rhine at Wesel.

The 370th FG returned to the USA in October 1945 and, re-designated the 140th Fighter Group, was assigned to the Colorado Air National Guard. It was called to active duty in Tactical Air Command on 1 April 1951, during the Korean War and, as the 140th Fighter-Bomber Group, continued to use Mustangs until the following year.

Apart from the units mentioned above, some Eighth Air Force Mustang groups were placed under the operational control of the Ninth Air Force during the crucial period of the Battle of the Bulge. They included the 339th, 352nd, 361st and 479th Fighter Groups. Based at Fowlmere, the 339th FG had the remarkable distinction of being awarded two Distinguished Unit Citations within forty-eight hours, the first for an attack on Erding airfield during a bomber escort mission on 10 September 1944 and the second for another strafing attack on an airfield near Karlsruhe the next day. The group provided fighter cover for transport during the airborne landings at Arnhem and Nijmegen, flew numerous offensive patrols during the Ardennes battle and covered the Rhine crossing. In the course of 264 operations, the 339th FG claimed more than 200 enemy aircraft destroyed in air combat and 400 on the ground. The group returned to the USA in October 1945.

The 352nd Fighter Group at Bodney in Norfolk, whose P-51s had flown many ground attack sorties in support of the D-Day landings, the St Lo breakout and the operations around Arnhem, rotated its squadrons to Asch, in Belgium, under Ninth Air Force control during the Ardennes offensive. On New Year's Day 1945, the group was lucky enough to be airborne when the enemy launched Operation *Bodenplatte*, the massive air strike against Allied airfields in the Low Countries. When Asch was attacked by some fifty Focke-Wulfs and Messerschmitts, the Mustangs fell on them and destroyed almost half the attacking force for no loss. Most of the damage was caused by the 487th Squadron, led by Lt Col John C. Meyer, who shot

P-51D of an unidentified unit in England, 1944, displays a rather poignant message on its nose.

down two enemy aircraft in the engagement. Captains Sanford Moats and William T. Whisner destroyed four each. For this action, the 487th FS was awarded a Distinguished Unit Citation.

The task of the Eighth Air Force Mustang groups sent to Belgium during the Ardennes offensive was to provide continuous front line area patrol, with one squadron airborne, one ready to take off and replace the first, and the third on readiness. Bad weather severely curtailed operations, but during the infrequent clear spells there was plenty of action. On Christmas Day 1944, for example, the 479th Fighter Group destroyed seventeen enemy aircraft in its biggest air battle of the war.

It was on this day that the 352nd Fighter Group suffered a grievous loss. Major George E. Preddy of the 328th FS was patrolling south-west of Coblenz with his squadron when he sighted two Messerschmitt 109s, which he chased and shot down; they were his 25th and 26th victims. Soon afterwards, near Liège, he saw a low-flying Fw 190 and went after it. The two aircraft ran into heavy American machine-gun fire. Preddy tried to break away, but he was too late. Moments later Preddy was killed when his Mustang plunged into the ground. He was the seventh-ranking USAAF ace of World War Two.

Chapter 6
Sicily, Italy and The Balkans

IN THE summer of 1943, two USAAF fighter-bomber groups in XII Air Support Command, Northwest African Air Forces, were equipped with Mustangs. These were the 27th Fighter-Bomber Group (522nd, 523rd and 524th FBS) and the 86th Fighter-Bomber Group (525th, 526th and 527th FBS), both of which were equipped with the A-36A. The 27th FBG began operations in June 1943, and the 86th FBG in the following month. Also in this theatre, the 111th Tactical Reconnaissance Squadron was equipped with P-51s, and in July 1943 the RAF formed No 1437 Strategic Reconnaissance Flight with Mustang Mk IIs, the latter unit forming part of No 285 Wing, Desert Air Force, alongside Nos 40 and 60 Squadrons, South African Air Force.

Both fighter-bomber groups were active in the air attacks preceding the Allied landings on Sicily, paying special attention to the airfield at Gerbini and its satellites on which the *Luftwaffe*'s fighters were concentrated. By the morning of D-Day, 9 July 1943, seven of these were unserviceable, and the air attacks switched to defensive positions and lines of communication. Casualties were heavy; between 1 and 18 July the two groups lost twenty A-36s. By 16 July both groups were installed at a newly-built advanced landing strip at Licata, on the island itself, from where they flew operations in support of the US Seventh Army.

Enemy resistance stiffened during the last week of July, with some of the bitterest fighting taking place at the town of Troina. At 1645 hours on 4 August, the softening-up of the town's defences began with an artillery bombardment and an air assault by seventy-two A-36s of the 27th and 86th FBG, each aircraft carrying a 500 lb bomb. US forces finally broke into the town on

Ground crew manhandling a 27th FBG A-36 into its sandbagged shelter on Sicily, 1943.

5 August, leaving the two A-36 groups free to support an assault by the US 7th Infantry on Monte Fratello. For thirteen-and-a-half hours the A-36s pounded the enemy positions on the high ground and also laid smoke to conceal the movements of the attacking troops, which took Monte Fratello on 8 August.

After the fall of Sicily the 27th and 86th FBG gave fighter-bomber support to the Allied landings at Salerno, on the Italian mainland, and moved to bases in Italy when the southern part of the country was secured. Both groups took part in the air assault on Monte Cassino in February 1944 and continued to support ground operations before re-equipping with P-47s some weeks later.

The 31st and 52nd Fighter groups, which had been equipped with Spitfire Vs during the North African campaign and which had taken these aircraft to Italy, began re-equipping with P-51D Mustangs in April 1944. Two more fighter groups, the 325th and 332nd, also re-equipped with Mustangs in May and June 1944 respectively. The 52nd FG was assigned to the tactical role with the Twelfth Air Force, the remainder

This A-36 was written off following a crash-landing at Tartantella, Sicily, after being hit by 88 mm flak.

to the Fifteenth Air Force, their primary task being bomber escort. One of the main strategic aims of the Fifteenth Air Force early in 1944 was to inflict as much damage as possible on that portion of the enemy's air power which could be brought to bear on the Italian war zone. Another aim was to delay the arrival of troop reinforcements from the Balkans. To this end Sofia was heavily bombed six times in two months, the Bulgarian capital being the hub of the German-controlled supply system for all south-eastern Europe. On 16 January B-17s struck for the first time against the Messerschmitt aircraft factory at Klagenfurt, lying in the Carinthian Alps some fourteen miles from the Yugoslav border. On the 30th the Fifteenth Air Force attacked airfields in north-east Italy at which enemy bombers arriving from the Balkans refuelled before taking off to bomb the Allied concentrations in the Anzio and Nettuno bridgeheads.

By this time the heavy bombers of the Fifteenth Air Force were concentrated on airfields around Foggia, in southern Italy, which brought them within easy range of many major targets which it had hitherto been impossible to attack. Nevertheless, it was some time before the strategic air offensive from Italy got into its full stride. It took a considerable time to build up at Foggia all the supplies and facilities necessary for the operation of a heavy bomber force, and during the winter of 1943-4 the weather over Italy was abysmal. With improved conditions in the spring, however, the Allied bombers renewed their day and night offensive against the enemy's oil resources in the Balkans, and this time the heavy bombers – which had hitherto relied on P-38 and P-47 escorts – had the Mustang groups to look after them.

On 21 April 1944 the 31st Fighter Group mounted its first 'big show' with the new Mustangs when it was detailed to escort a B-24 mission raiding the oil refineries at Ploesti, in Romania. The group's task was to meet the bombers after they had left the target area and escort them home. Near

P-51Bs of the 31st Fighter
Group in Italy, early 1944.

Bucharest the Mustang pilots sighted a formation of B-24s being attacked by at least sixty enemy fighters. Attacking out of the sun, the Americans took the enemy completely by surprise, and in the ensuing battle the 31st FG's pilots claimed seventeen enemy aircraft destroyed, seven probably destroyed and ten damaged for the loss of two of their own. It was a notable success which earned the group a Distinguished Unit Citation.

On 22 July, the 31st Fighter Group was once again detailed for an escort mission to Ploesti. While bomb-carrying P-38 Lightnings of the 82nd Group attacked the oil refinery installations, the Mustangs strafed a nearby airfield before going on to land at Piryatin in Russia. On 25 July, thirty-five Mustangs escorted the P-38s on a ground-attack mission to the German airfield at Mielec in Poland. During the return flight they encountered a formation of thirty-six Ju 87 Stukas, laden with bombs

South African AF Mustang Is in Italy, 1944.

and heading for the Russian lines. The Mustangs ripped in among the slow-flying dive-bombers and a frightful slaughter ensued. Within minutes the wreckage of twenty-seven Stukas was blazing on the ground. The destruction of an entire *Luftwaffe* dive-bomber wing earned the 31st FG its second Distinguished Unit Citation. On 26 July the Mustangs flew back to their bases in Italy.

P-51Ds of the 325th FG escorting B-17s on a raid into southern Germany.

Mustang IVs of No 213 Squadron, Italy, 1945.

The first RAF unit to equip with Mustangs in Italy was No 260 Squadron, which exchanged its Kittyhawks for Mustang IIIs at Cutella in April 1944. In May 1944 No 213 Squadron also converted to Mustang IIIs in Egypt, taking its aircraft to Italy for operations with the Balkan Air Force. The third RAF squadron to receive Mustang IIIs was No 112, which moved from Tunisia to Safi, Malta, in July 1944 and then to Tissano in Italy to provide air support for the Allied armies. September saw the conversion to Mustangs of No 249 Squadron, which had been flying fighter sweeps over Yugoslavia and Albania with Spitfire IXs from Canne, while No 3 Squadron Royal Australian Air Force and 5 Squadron South African Air Force exchanged their Kittyhawks for Mustangs in October 1944. Nos 3 RAAF, 112, 250 and 260 Squadrons formed part of No 239 Wing, alongside the Kittyhawks of No 450 Squadron, RAAF.

In July 1944 the fighter-bomber groups of the USAAF XII Tactical Air Command (as the former Air Support Command was now known) moved to Corsica in readiness to support the forthcoming Allied invasion of southern France, code-named Operation *Dragoon*. Consequently, the RAF Desert Air Force was left to provide close air support along the whole Italian front. With the invasion successfully concluded, the

Tactical Air Command returned to Italy to assume, under the name of XII Fighter Command, control of operations in close support of the US Fifth Army, and on 20 September 1944 the Desert Air Force returned to support the British Eighth Army and the eastern sector of the front.

Mustang IV of No 112 Squadron, bearing the unit's distinctive shark's teeth markings.

From June 1944 the RAF's long-range Mustangs were assigned to the support of the newly-formed Balkan Air Force, Nos 112 and 260 Squadrons moving to Crete for this purpose in July. Other Mustang squadrons operated in support of Marshal Tito's Yugoslavian partisan forces, carrying out attacks against rail traffic on the main Zagreb-Belgrade-Skopje line, running down the peninsula into Greece, and also the coastal line through Brod-Sarajevo-Mostar. In the first month of operation the

Mustang IVs of No 213 Squadron, pictured in Italy in 1945.

Mustangs, together with Balkan Air Force Spitfires, claimed an impressive total of 262 locomotives destroyed or damaged, of which about a third were pulling troop trains.

In mid-July the Germans launched a determined attack against the Partisan II Corps in Montenegro, converging movements from the east and north being supported by a force of between twenty and thirty Junkers Ju 87s and Fiesler Fi 156 Storches. The Partisans counter-attacked vigorously with the support of Spitfires and Mustangs of the Balkan Air Force, and the enemy offensive was halted within a few days. The Mustang squadron involved in these operations was No 213, its aircraft flying from Biferno on the east coast of Italy. The same squadron continued to support the Partisans during August and September 1944, and on 23 August it provided fighter escort for Dakota aircraft of the 60th Troop Carrier Group, USAAF, and 267 Squadron RAF, which flew to a landing strip near Brezna, Yugoslavia, and evacuated 1,078 wounded Partisans. The squadron also flew a number of fighter sweeps over Greece during this period. Losses were heavy; between 7 July and 31 October No 213 Squadron lost twenty-five Mustangs. Three were due to accidental causes; the others were the victims of flak, with two notable exceptions. These were HB888, which flew into the ground while attacking a Savoia-Marchetti SM79 near Crepaja, Yugoslavia, on 13 September, and KH554, which was hit by return fire from a Fiesler Storch (which the Mustang pilot no doubt considered easy game) and destroyed in a forced landing near Martinka Ves, Yugoslavia, on 10 October. In fact, this was the only RAF Mustang III shot down by an enemy aircraft in the entire Italian campaign, although KH616 of No 3 Squadron RAAF had to be abandoned after being damaged by a Messerschmitt 109 on 26 December.

Early in September 1944, the whole situation in the Balkans underwent a complete change when two of Germany's allies, Bulgaria and Romania – threatened with massive destruction by the advancing Soviet armies – changed sides and declared war on their erstwhile partner. Immediately, the pressure on the Partisans in Montenegro was lifted. Another consequence was that the continued occupation of Greece and the Aegean Islands became impossible for the Germans, and their evacuation a difficult and hazardous undertaking.

Before that, RAF Mustangs had played their part in the Allied offensive against enemy forces in the Aegean, where the bombers and fighter-bombers of No 201 Group were intensely active against enemy shipping in the spring and summer of 1944. By the end of May, the position of the German garrison in Crete was becoming serious. They desperately needed supplies, and on the last day of the month three laden freighters sailed from Athens escorted by four destroyers, four corvettes and two E-Boats, all under an air umbrella of Messerschmitt 109s and Arado 196 floatplanes. The ships were constantly shadowed by reconnaissance aircraft, and in the early evening of 1 June, when they were twenty-seven miles north of Iraklion, they were attacked by a strong force of RAF and SAAF Baltimores, Marauders and Beaufighters escorted by thirteen Spitfires and four Mustangs, the latter from No 260 Squadron. After the attack two of the freighters were stationary in the water and a third was burning fiercely, being abandoned by its crew.

Early the next morning, two Mustangs of No 260 Squadron discovered that one of the freighters hit during the attack had reached Iraklion harbour, where she was on fire; a second air strike finished her off, together with one of the escorting destroyers.

While the RAF, RAAF and SAAF Mustang squadrons continued to support Allied ground operations in Italy and the Balkans, the P-51Ds of the Fifteenth Air Force's 31st, 52nd, 325th and 332nd Fighter Groups ranged far and wide across southern Europe on their bomber escort missions, accompanying B-17s and B-24s to targets in northern Italy, France, Poland, Czechoslovakia, Romania, Austria, Hungary, Bulgaria, Yugoslavia and Greece. The top-scoring Mustang pilot of the Fifteenth Air Force was Lt John J. Voll of the 31st Fighter Group, with twenty-one victories. According to Voll, one of the most formidable enemy aircraft he encountered was a Macchi 202, flown by a pilot of the Fascist *Aeronautica Nazionale Repubblicana*, which became his thirteenth victory on 23 September 1944. This is his combat report of the encounter:

'On our way home I saw a Macchi 202 through a break in the clouds and went after him. Going in and out of the cloud I was chasing his vapor trail rather than actually seeing him all the time and when I finally got into position to fire I glanced behind me and there was another Macchi on my tail. I started firing and although I only used up twenty rounds per gun on the Macchi in front of me, it seemed as though I had used a hundred before my hits blew the cockpit apart and the pilot bailed out. I started to attack the other plane, but by this time another had joined the fight. Since the Macchi can turn a shade sharper than a Mustang, they soon had me boxed. I got into a cloud and headed home.'

Mustang of No 213 Squadron, at low level over Italy in 1945.

Another pilot of the 31st FG who had trouble with the nimble Italian fighters was Captain Jim Brooks. On one mission he sighted about ten enemy fighters high to starboard, approaching fast, and called his flight leader to break hard into them, but the transmission went unheard and Brooks found himself fighting the enemy single-handed.

'There were Fw 190s, Me 109s, a Macchi 202 and an Italian fighter similar to the 109. They had me so hopelessly out-numbered that one Fw 190 had his gear down, for what reason I don't know. He did make a head-on pass, firing as he came. However, he was of little concern to me at the time as the Macchi had latched onto me and wouldn't turn me loose. The radius of turn of the Macchi is a great deal better than a Mustang and we went around three turns in a Lufbery circle. I knew about the fourth or fifth turn he would be able to pull his nose around and be in a good position to fire, so I split-essed and fortunately he did not follow.'

Brooks destroyed thirteen enemy aircraft during his time with the 31st FG, four of them on 26 June 1944. Another Fifteenth Air Force Mustang pilot with thirteen victories was Captain Harry A. Parker of the 325th Fighter Group, who also destroyed four enemy aircraft – all Bf 109s – on 30th July 1944.

The Italian ANR pilots were no mean opponents, although most of their successes were registered against P-38s, P-47s and Spitfires. They generally flew in mixed groups with *Luftwaffe* fighters, which occasionally presented problems; on 29 April 1944, for example, Bf 109Gs of JG 77 bounced an Italian formation, mistaking its Macchi C.205s for Mustangs, and shot two of them down.

On 22 December 1944 the 31st Fighter Group scored the Fifteenth Air Force's first jet kill when a Messerschmitt Me 262 was shot down by Lts Eugene P. McGlauflin and Roy L. Scales during a photo-reconnaissance mission. The second time the 31st FG's Mustangs encountered German jets was on 22 March 1945, when a lone Me 262 was destroyed by Captain William L. Dillard during an escort mission to Ruhland. Then, on 24 March, came a grand finale for the Fifteenth Air Force when the 31st FG destroyed no fewer than five Me 262s while escorting heavy bombers to Berlin.

For the RAF and USAAF Mustang squadrons, the campaign in Italy and the Balkans never received the same glamour –

Mustang IV of No 213 Squadron at Nicosia, Cyprus, in 1946.

if that is the right word to use – as the operations in north-west Europe. It was, to use the infantryman's term, a 'hard slog' from start to finish, with weather conditions ranging from boiling dust and blistering heat through torrential rain and mud to freezing snow.

Close support operations in Italy and the Balkans cost the RAF, RAAF and SAAF squadrons 161 Mustang IIIs, the great majority falling to flak, in about a year of operations. Some of the squadrons were just beginning to convert to Mustang IVs when hostilities ceased in May 1945.

Chapter 7
Mustang Escort: By Daylight to Germany, June 1944–May 1945

T HE SUMMER of 1944 saw the launching of Project Frantic, which was designed to enable American bombers to strike at targets which had previously been out of range. The basic idea was that the bombers, operating from bases in Britain or Italy, would bomb selected targets on the outward strip, land in Russia to refuel and rearm, then strike at other targets on their way home. As a secondary aim, it was hoped that these 'shuttle bombing' operations would force the *Luftwaffe* to disperse its already overstretched resources still further in an effort to meet the new attacks over a larger strategic area made up of German-held Polish territory.

Negotiations began in December 1943, but it was not until the following April that the Russians finally agreed to the use of their bases by American aircraft, and even then they allocated only three airfields

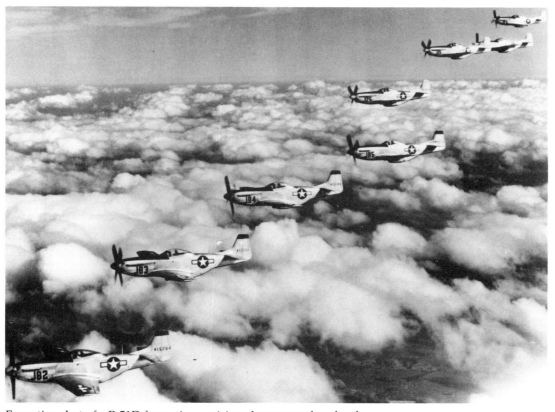

Evocative shot of a P-51D formation cruising above cumulus clouds.

P-51D of the 31st FG displays twelve 'kills' below the cockpit.

instead of the six required. All three airfields lay in the devastated 'scorched earth' area around Kiev, and throughout April and May 1944 American engineers worked hard to extend runways, build new base facilities and generally get the fields into shape. Of the three, only Poltava was really suitable for handling heavy bombers; Mirgorod could accommodate only a few, while Piryatin was just big enough to be used by fighters.

Project Frantic was eventually launched on 2 June 1944, when thirty B-17s and seventy P-51s of the Fifteenth Air Force took off from their Italian bases, bombed the marshalling yards at Debrecen and flew on to the airfields in Russia. From there, on 6 June, they struck at the airfield of Galatz in Romania, and on the 10th, on their way back to Italy, they also bombed the Romanian airfield at Foscani. Only two B-17s and two Mustangs were lost in the three operations.

On 21 June 1944 it was the turn of the Eighth Air Force, when 163 B-17s were briefed to attack oil installations at Ruhland/Schwarzenheide and then fly on to the airfields of Poltava and Piryatin. The escort force was provided by sixty-one Mustangs of the Fourth Fighter Group and

one squadron of the 352nd Fighter Group, the 486th FS, all led by Don Blakeslee. Even for the Mustang it was a long way to go, involving seven-and-a-half hours in the cockpit, and there was little fuel margin for combat. The operation was part of a much bigger effort, with other bomber formations attacking targets elsewhere.

The Mustangs made their rendezvous with the bombers over Leszlo, in Poland, after the B-17s had bombed their targets and escorted them towards the Russian frontier. En route the formation was attacked from head-on by twenty-five Bf 109s which were held off with some difficulty, as the Mustang pilots could not indulge in fuel-consuming combat manoeuvres. Two 109s and one Mustang were shot down. The P-51s landed at Piryatin on schedule, leaving the B-17s to fly on to Poltava with an escort of Russian Yak fighters. What the American crews did not know was that, as they droned high over eastern Europe, they had been shadowed by a lone Heinkel He 177 long-range bomber. As darkness fell, eighty Junkers 88s and Heinkel 111s of General Rudolf Meister's Fourth *Fleigerkorps* took off from airfields behind German lines and headed east. At 2335 hrs Russian authorities warned the American HQ staff at Poltava that enemy aircraft had crossed the front line and were reported to be heading for the Kiev area. The alert was sounded and Allied personnel on the three 'Frantic' airfields took off.

A few minutes after midnight, flares cascaded down on Poltava and the Flying Fortresses, only one of which was camouflaged, stood out vividly. More flares were dropped during the next ten minutes. The Russian anti-aircraft batteries put up a furious barrage but failed to hit anything. Then the first bombs fell. For an hour Poltava was pounded incessantly by the enemy bombers, which bombed singly from altitudes up to 10,000 feet. The last wave, consisting entirely of Ju 88s, swept over the field at low level, raking it with cannon and machine-gun fire.

When the last of the bombers departed, the airfield at Poltava was littered with the wreckage of forty-seven B-17s, and every one of the remaining bombers was

P-51D 'Rugged Rebel' of the 364th FG, after landing short of the runway at Honington, Suffolk, on 17 October 1944.

P-51Ds of the 364th FG at Honington. The three aircraft have been involved in a taxying accident, one losing its wingtip and the other its tail unit.

damaged. Nearly half a million gallons of petrol had gone up in flames. Thirty Russians and two Americans had been killed, and a hundred Allied personnel wounded. Not a single German aircraft had been lost. The Poltava disaster, taken together with the casualties suffered by VIII Bomber Command in action over Germany that day, represented an overall loss of ninety-one aircraft, the highest ever sustained by Eighth Air Force in a twenty-four hour period. Never again would the *Luftwaffe* achieve so much in a single blow.

On 22 June the Mustangs were dispersed from Piryatin in case of another attack, and it was another four days before Blakeslee led his aircraft on the first leg of the flight back to Debden, via Foggia in Italy. On 2 July, the 4th FG joined Mustangs of the Fifteenth Air Force on a mission to Budapest and lost five aircraft to spirited fighter resistance. One of the missing pilots was Captain Ralph Hofer, who a year earlier had become one of the 56th Fighter Group's first aces while flying Thunderbolts. On 5 July the 4th FG's Mustangs returned to England with another shuttle-bombing mission, having operated over ten countries and logged 6,000 miles in twenty-nine-and-a-half hours of operational flying. The group had claimed ten enemy aircraft destroyed for the loss of seven Mustangs. The shuttle bombing tactics continued on and off for the next few months before being dropped for good.

On 28 July 1944 Mustang pilots of the 359th Fighter Group were on an escort mission over Merseburg when they encountered a new and alarming development: the Messerschmitt Me 163 rocket-propelled fighter. What happened is described in the combat report of the group's commander, Colonel Avelin P. Tacon, Jr, who erroneously described the enemy aircraft as jet-propelled.

'My eight P-51s were furnishing close escort for a combat wing of B-17s, and we were flying south at 25,000 ft when one of my pilots called in two contrails at six o'clock high some five miles back at 32,000 ft. I identified them immediately as jet-propelled aircraft. Their contrails could not be mistaken and looked very dense and white, somewhat like an elongated cumulus cloud some three-quarters of a mile in length. My section turned 180 degrees back towards the enemy fighters, which included two with jets turned on and three in a glide without jets operating at the moment.

Colonel John C. Meyer, top-scoring ace of the 352nd FG.

'The two I had spotted made a diving turn to the left in close formation and feinted toward the bombers at six o'clock, cutting off their jets as they turned. Our flight turned for a head-on pass to get between them and the rear of the bomber formation. While still 3,000 yds from the bombers, they turned into us and let the bombers alone. In this turn they banked about eighty degrees but their course changed only about twenty degrees.

'Their turn radius was very large but their rate of roll appeared excellent. Their speed I estimated was 500 to 600 miles per hour. Both planes passed under us, 1,000 ft below, while still in a close formation glide. In an attempt to follow them, I split-S'd. One continued down in a forty-five degree dive, the other climbed up into the sun very steeply and I lost him. Then I looked away at the one in a dive and saw that he was five miles away at 10,000 ft. Other members of my flight said that the one who went into the sun used his jets in short bursts as though blowing smoke rings. These pilots appeared very experienced but not aggressive. Maybe they were just on a trial flight.'

have to be in positions relatively close to the bombers to be between them and our heavies. It is believed that these tactics will keep them from making effective, repeat effective, attacks on the bombers. Attention is called to the fact that probably the first thing that will be seen will be heavy, dense contrails high and probably 30,000 ft above approaching rear of bombers. Jet aircraft can especially be expected in Leipzig and Munich area or any place east of nine degree line.'

The Me 163s put in another appearance on 5 August 1944, and this time the VIII FC Mustang pilots, escorting B-17s over Magdeburg, were made brutally aware of

The appearance of the Messerschmitt 262 caused VIIIth Fighter Command to revise its escort tactics.

The encounter brought an immediate reaction from HQ VIII Fighter Command, which issued a circular to all units.

'It is believed we can expect to see more of these aircraft immediately and that we can expect attacks on the bombers from the rear in formations or waves. To be able to encounter and have time to turn into them our units are going to

the rocket fighter's potential. The Me 163s dived on the P-51s in line astern and opened fire with their 30mm cannon. The Mustangs broke hard to meet the attack, but they were too late; three of them were shot down and the Me 163s had vanished almost before the other American pilots realised what was happening. On 16 August, however, the Mustang pilots proved that the *Luftwaffe*'s new weapon

P-51D of the 52nd Fighter Group, over Italy.

had not made the propeller-driven aircraft completely obsolete when a pair of P-51s destroyed two 163s which were attacking a straggling B-17.

On 6 August 1944 one of VIII Fighter Command's top-scoring Mustang pilots, Captain George Preddy of the 352nd Fighter Group, had a particularly outstanding day. His combat report tells the story.

'We were escorting the lead combat wings of B-17s when thirty-plus Me 109s in formation came into the third box from the south. We were 1,000 feet above them so I led White Flight, consisting of Lieutenant Heyer, Lieutenant Doleac and myself, in astern of them. I opened fire on one near the rear of the formation from 300 yds dead astern and got many hits around the cockpit. The enemy aircraft went down inverted and in flames.

'At this time Lieutenant Doleac became lost while shooting down an Me 109 that had gotten on Lieutenant Heyer's tail. Lieutenant Heyer and I continued our attack and I drove up

behind another enemy aircraft, getting hits around the wing roots and setting him on fire after a short burst. He went spinning down and the pilot baled out at 20,000 ft. I then saw Lieutenant Heyer on my right shooting down another enemy aircraft.

'The enemy formation stayed together taking practically no evasive action and tried to get back for an attack on the bombers who were off to the right. We continued with our attack on the rear end and I fired on another from close range. He went down smoking badly and I saw him begin to fall apart below us.

P-51D of the 350 FS, 353rd FG, after a crash landing at Raydon, December 1944.

'At this time four other P-51s came in to help us with the attack. I fired at another 109, causing him to burn after a short burst. He spiralled down to the right in flames. The formation headed down a left turn, keeping themselves together in rather close formation. I got a good burst at another one causing him to burn and spin down. The enemy aircraft were down to 5,000 ft now and one pulled off to the left. I was all alone with them now, so I went after this single 109 before he could get on my tail. I got in an ineffective burst causing him to smoke a little. I pulled up into a steep climb to the left above him and he climbed after me. I pulled it in as tight as possible and climbed at about 150 miles per hour. The Hun opened fire on me but could not get enough deflection to do any damage. With my initial speed I slightly out-climbed him. He fell off to the left and I dropped down astern of him. He jettisoned his canopy as I fired a short burst getting many hits. As I pulled past, the pilot baled out at 7,000 ft.

'I lost contact with all friendly and enemy aircraft so I headed home alone.

CLAIM: Six (6) Me 109s.'

For this feat Preddy received the Distinguished Service Cross, the USA's second highest decoration. Soon afterwards he went home on leave, returning to the 352nd FG in November. On Christmas Day, he was flying south-west of Coblenz when he sighted two Me 109s, which he chased and shot down; they were his twenty-fifth and twenty-sixth victims. A few minutes later, near Liège, he saw a low-flying Fw 190 and went after it. The two aircraft ran into intense American anti-aircraft fire. Preddy crash-landed his Mustang, but he had been hit by several .50 bullets and was killed.

On 28 August 1944, Eighth Air Force Thunderbolt pilots shot down a Messerschmitt 262 jet fighter near Termonde, Belgium, in the Americans' first recorded encounter with this new type. With its greater endurance and four 30mm cannon, the Me 262 was a far more formidable opponent than the rocket-powered Me 163, but even so it was by no means invincible. On 7 October, Lieutenant Urban Drew of the 361st FG, flying a Mustang, destroyed two of the enemy jets as they were taking off from Achmer.

Most of the VIII Fighter Command's activities during September 1944 were devoted to strafing attacks on enemy rolling stock and road transport, and also to flak suppression in the Arnhem and Nijmegen areas in support of the airborne landings. There were also some very successful airfield attacks, notably on 5 September, when Mustangs of the 55th FG's 343rd Fighter Squadron attacked enemy aircraft taking off from Goppingen

Ground crews jack up a P-51D of the 353rd FG after the aircraft ran into soft ground at Raydon, December 1944.

A rather battered P-51D of the 78th FG, after a forced landing at Duxford, May 1945.

and destroyed sixteen for no loss. For this, and other successful missions during a nine-day operational period, the 55th FG received a Distinguished Unit Citation.

Airfield attacks were intensified during November 1944, the Mustangs joining other Allied types – notably the RAF's Tempests – in seeking out the elusive Me 262s, which were becoming increasingly troublesome. At this stage the enemy jets were mainly employed in carrying out low-level attacks on Allied installations and armoured columns, but one of the most important tasks was fast low-level reconnaissance. For months, the jets roved virtually at will over the entire battlefront, photographing

This P-51D of the 354th FG turned over on its back after a tyre burst. The pilot escaped unhurt.

installations deep behind the Allied lines and gradually enabling the German General Staff to build up a complete intelligence picture of the Allied order of battle in northern France, Holland and Belgium. Slipping over the front line at zero feet and hugging the contours of the terrain, the 262s usually achieved complete surprise and completed their missions before the Allied defences were able to react.

Different sets of tactics were adopted to counter the 262 threat. The Hawker Tempest Vs of the RAF's No 122 Wing, the only Allied aircraft with any hope of catching the jets by any other means than a high-speed dive, operated in pairs at low and medium level, with a second pair held in readiness on the ground. The USAAF's Mustangs, in contrast, patrolled at about 10,000 feet, so that if a 262 was sighted the Mustang's high acceleration in the dive could be used to good advantage. More often than not, however, the expertly camouflaged 262s, which were extremely difficult to spot from a higher altitude, eluded this fighter screen and got clean away.

The operational debut of the Arado Ar 234 jet bomber/reconnaissance aircraft in the late summer of 1944 released some of the *Luftwaffe*'s Me 262 fleet for interceptor duties, and an experimental Me 262 fighter unit was formed at Lechfeld, near Augsberg. It was originally commanded by *Hauptmann* Tierfelder, who was killed when his aircraft crashed in flames during one of the unit's early operational missions. His successor was Major Walter Nowotny, who, at the age of twenty-three, was one of the *Luftwaffe*'s top fighter pilots with 258 kills, almost all of them scored on the Eastern front. By the end of October the *Kommando* Nowotny, as the unit had come to be known, had reached full operational status and was transferred to the airfields of Achmer and Hesepe near Osnabrück, astride the main American daylight bomber approach route.

Because of a shortage of adequately trained pilots and technical problems, the *Kommando* Nowotny was usually only able to fly three or four sorties a day against the enemy formations, yet in November 1944 the pilots destroyed twenty-two aircraft. By the end of the month, however, the unit had only three serviceable aircraft out of a total of thirty on strength, a rate of attrition accounted for mainly by accidents rather than enemy action. It had also lost its talented commander.

On 8 November 1944, Walter Nowotny was the pilot of one of five Me 262s which took off to attack an American bomber formation. Operating from the 262 bases was now a very hazardous operation since the Allies had pinpointed their locations, and for several days they had been subjected to heavy attacks by fighter-bombers. Additional 20mm flak batteries were hastily brought up and organized into flak lanes, extending for two miles outwards from the ends of the main runways to provide a curtain of fire during the jet fighter's critical take-off and landing phases. For additional protection, a *Gruppe* of Focke-Wulf 190D fighters (III/JG 54) was assigned to the air defence of Achmer and Hesepe.

On this November morning, in the operations room at Achmer, the German controllers followed the course of the air battle that developed over Germany. They heard Nowotny claim a victory, and also heard one of the other Me 262 pilots state that he was being shot down by Mustangs. A few minutes later, Nowotny came on the air again to report that his port engine had failed and that he was coming in to make an emergency landing. Some time later, his 262 was sighted on the approach some four miles away from Achmer with wheels and flaps down and at least six Mustangs behind it. The observers on the ground saw Nowotny's undercarriage come up and the aircraft enter a steep climbing turn on one engine. He had obviously decided to fight it out rather than continue his approach, which would have been suicidal. A few seconds passed, then the watchers saw the

In the closing stages of the war, Mustang pilots ranging over Germany added aircraft like this 'Mistel' combination to their scores.

262 disappear behind a low hill. There was an explosion, followed by a column of black smoke. The Mustangs climbed away pursued by scattering bursts of flak, leaving the wreckage of Nowotny's 262 burning in a field near the village of Bremsche.

Soon after Nowotny's death, the jet fighter *Kommando* returned to Lechfeld for further training. Most of the pilots had only ten hours' experience on the Me 262, and the air battles had shown that not even the jet fighter's superior speed would compensate for the lack of experience when confronted with veteran Allied fighter pilots. Unfamiliarity with the high-speed aircraft led to a number of combat losses when Me 262 pilots, finding that they were overshooting their target, throttled back and so lost their superior speed advantage.

The Eighth Air Force took the Me 262 threat very seriously indeed, and VIII Fighter Command modified its tactics to counter it. The size of the fighter escort was increased so that every pair of bombers had a Mustang escorting them, so that

eventually the number of fighters in each group reached a peak of 135 aircraft. The established practice was maintained whereby the groups operated in two separate A and B formations, each with three squadrons of twelve aircraft, and wherever possible steps were taken to ensure that the fighter groups had a height advantage so that they could use their diving speed to intercept the attacking 262s.

Meanwhile, in October, soon after the extent of the Me 262 threat had been realised, Eighth Air Force had asked the RAF for some assistance with jet fighter affiliation, and a programme of air exercises took place. It lasted a week, from 10–17 October, with four Gloster Meteors of No 616 Squadron RAF visiting Debden. On 10 October, 120 B-24s and B-17s of the Second Bombardment Division took off from their respective bases and made rendezvous with their fighter escort of Mustangs at 9,000 feet over Peterborough. In four tight boxes they set out over the exercise route, flying from Peterborough to

Colchester, back to Peterborough, then heading north-west before finally turning on a reciprocal course towards East Anglia.

During the flight the four Meteors made a series of high-speed attacks on the formation, closing from various angles at 450 knots IAS and passing through the bomber boxes before the fighter escorts had time to react. The only way to catch the jets was to step up the fighter escort at least 5,000 feet above the bombers, which enabled the Mustangs to build up speed by half rolling and diving in pursuit. This method, however, involved very precise timing, and even if the Meteors were intercepted they were usually able to escape by virtue of their higher speed. Nevertheless, by the end of the week the Mustang pilots were achieving successful interceptions more frequently, and valuable points on potential defensive measures were raised at the debriefing which followed each exercise.

In practice, over Germany, the outcome of an encounter with the Me 262s depended very much on which side had the tactical advantage of height. Two of the enemy jet fighters were shot down on 6 November because the American pilots enjoyed a height advantage. One of the Mustang pilots was Captain Charles Yeager of the 357th Fighter Group, who was leading a flight of Mustangs north of Osnabrück when three Me 262s were sighted, flying on an opposite heading to the Mustangs and at two o'clock low. The Mustangs dived down from 10,000 feet and Yeager attacked the last jet in the trio, scoring some hits before the 262s pulled away. A few moments later he sighted the 262s again, flying an overcast, and fired a high-deflection burst at the leader. Again he scored hits, and again the 262s used their superior speed to get away. Then, a few more minutes into his patrol, Yeager spotted another 262 approaching to land at an airfield. Braving intense flak, he dived down at 500 mph and fired a short burst into the 262's wing. The jet crash-landed short of the airfield, its wing shearing off.

A couple of weeks earlier, 'Chuck' Yeager had destroyed five Me 109s in a single sortie. He ended the war with eleven-and-a-half confirmed victories, and later became famous for his supersonic flights in the Bell X-1 series of rocket-powered research aircraft.

Bad weather hampered daylight bombing operations in mid-November 1944, but on the 21st the Eighth Air Force launched 1,291 B-17s against Germany, principally against Merseburg. All the Mustang groups were operating, and accounted for most of the 954 escort fighters despatched. The raid was bitterly contested by the *Luftwaffe*, who put up an estimated 300 fighters, mainly Fw 190s. In the ensuing air battles, somewhat hampered by cloud cover, top honours went to the 352nd Fighter Group with nineteen-and-a-half victories, the 364th with eighteen and the 359th with seventeen. The *Luftwaffe*'s fighters were again up in strength on 26 November, when VIII Bomber Command attacked oil supplies in the Hanover area. The enemy suffered heavy losses, the Mustangs claiming 114 enemy aircraft destroyed. Top-scoring group was the 339th, with twenty-nine – five of which were shot down by Lieutenant Jack Daniels – and was closely followed by the 356th FG, which claimed twenty-six. This kind of attrition was to be the pattern when the *Luftwaffe* challenged further raids during the remainder of November and early December. Then, suddenly, the enemy vanished from the sky.

The reason became apparent on 16 December, when the Germans launched their offensive in the Ardennes. Because of bad weather, it was not until 24 December that the Allies could mount a sizeable air effort, but on that day the Eighth Air Force despatched no fewer than 2,046 heavy bombers, escorted by 853 fighters from all groups except two (the 78th, in the process of converting from Thunderbolts to Mustangs, and the 339th, prevented from taking off from Duxford and Fowlmere because of dense fog). Together with substantial contributions from the Ninth

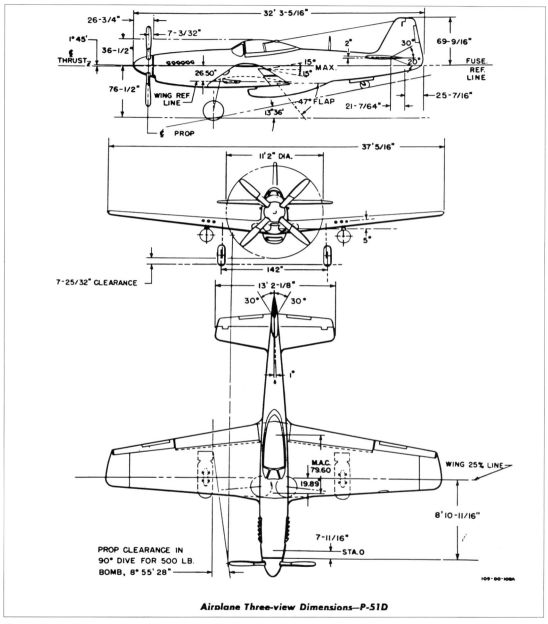

Airplane Three-view Dimensions—P-51D

General arrangement drawing of the P-51D Mustang.

AF and the RAF 2nd TAF, this was the largest air strike of the Second World War. The *Luftwaffe* came up to intercept, but the escorting fighters claimed the destruction of seventy-four enemy aircraft for the loss of ten of their own.

While some Eighth AF Mustang groups deployed to Belgium to assist the Ninth AF in ground-attack work during the Allied counter-offensive (see Chapter Five), the remainder continued to escort the B-17s and B-24s which, in January, were pounding the enemy's lines of supply and communication. There was bitter air fighting on 14 January, when B-24s and B-17s of the 2nd and 3rd Divisions attacked oil targets in the Magdeburg-Brunswick area. Prior to this, the British *Ultra* intelligence system at Bletchley Park had indicated that the German *Jagdverbände* would be employing new tactics involving frontal attacks in line abreast by heavily-armoured Fw 190s. The report was correct, and an estimated 300 enemy fighters took to the air. In the ensuing air battles the 357th Fighter Group, which put up a force of sixty-six Mustangs, was particularly successful, claiming the destruction of fifty-six-and-a-half enemy aircraft destroyed. The fight was typical of many others at this stage of the war, when the experience of Allied fighter pilots gave them an enormous advantage over their adversaries, the bulk of whom were thrown into battle with little training. The 357th FG's score that day was never surpassed,

and brought the Group a Distinguished Unit Citation.

In the early weeks of 1945, although the *Luftwaffe* was now at its last gasp, Allied fighter pilots began to encounter an extraordinary variety of targets as they ranged over Germany. New fighter types included the Focke-Wulf Fw 190D and the Ta 152H, the latter serving only in small numbers; both were assigned mainly to the protection of the Me 262 bases, and although both could meet the P-51D Mustang on equal terms (or better terms, in the case of the Ta 152H) it was the greater experience of the American pilots that usually decided the outcome of air combat.

The Me 262s were very active during February 1945, with Eighth AF bomber crews reporting 163 encounters with the jets and escorting Mustang pilots 118. Most of the 262s belonged to the newly-formed JG 7 'Hindenburg' *Jagdgeschwader*, commanded by Oberst Johannes Steinhoff. Although JG 7 eventually comprised three *Gruppen*, only one of these, III/JG 7, made real and continual contact with the enemy, moving in turn to bases at Brandenburg-Briest, Oranienburg and Parchim. Attacks

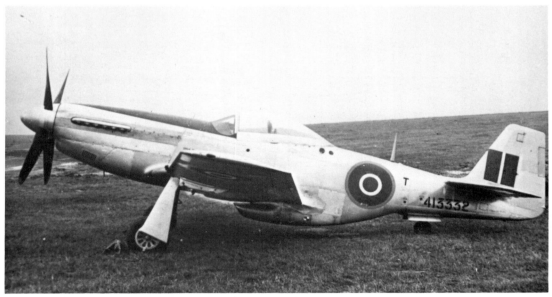

P-51D in RAF markings prior to delivery as Mustang IV. The aircraft still bears its US serial.

were usually made by units of *Staffel* (squadron) size, consisting of nine aircraft in three elements of three, employing the 'vic' formation with one aircraft leading and the other two on the flanks, slightly higher up and to the rear. If more than one *Staffel* was used the other *Staffel* flew on both sides to the rear and slightly higher, or to one side in echelon. Because of the jets' high speed there was no need for top cover. Once the bomber formation had been sighted, each *Staffel* commander selected an individual bomber group, beginning the attack run from a distance of 5,000 yards and 5,000 feet higher up. On the approach, the basic three-aircraft elements of the *Staffel* went into line astern, diving to a point some 1,500 feet below and 1,500 yards behind the bombers to gain speed before pulling up and flying straight and level for the last 1,000 yards. On the last stage of the attack the 262s reached a speed of about 530 mph, more than enough to avoid the Allied fighter escort.

In addition to the 262's normal Revi gunsight, which was used in conjunction with the 30mm cannon, each aircraft had graduations etched on its windscreen, spaced so as to frame the wingspan of a B-17 at a range of 650 yards, at which point a salvo of R4M rockets was launched. (III/JG received its first batch of these in mid-February 1945.) When the salvo was fired it spread out rather like a charge from a shotgun, increasing the chances of hitting one or more targets. Immediately the rockets were discharged the 262 pilot would open up with his cannon, closing in to 150 yards before breaking off. Taking full advantage of the 262's high speed, the German pilots would sweep low across the top of a bomber formation in a flat climb, either attacking a second formation or diving away if the Allied fighter escort was too close for comfort. Pilots were discouraged from flying underneath the bomber formation after an attack, as there was a danger of debris being sucked into the jet intakes. Since the 262's endurance was strictly limited, the pilots usually

headed for home after one firing pass.

The enemy jet activity in February 1945 began on the 9th, when about twelve Me 262s attacked a bomber formation in the Fulda area, north of Frankfurt. Mustang pilots of the 78th, 357th and 359th Fighter Groups claimed four kills and one probable. The Mustangs claimed three more 262s on 22 February, when the Allied air forces carried out Operation *Clarion*, a major attack on enemy marshalling yards, but the really big day for VIII Fighter Command came on the 25th, when the Mustang pilots destroyed no fewer than eight Me 262s and one Arado Ar 234 jet bomber.

This aircraft, and seven of the Me 262s, were destroyed by pilots of the 55th Fighter Group during a fighter sweep in the vicinity of Giebelstadt airfield. Two of the 262s were destroyed by Captain Donald Cummings, as his combat report reveals.

'I was leading Hellcat Yellow Flight on a fighter sweep at 10,000 ft in the vicinity of Giebelstadt A/D when several Me 262s were called in at nine o'clock, taking off from the field. Captain Penn, the squadron leader, ordered us to drop our tanks and engage the enemy.

'I peeled off from 11,000 ft, making a 180 degree turn to the left in a seventy degree dive after a jet which was then approaching the airdrome. I commenced firing from approximately 1,000 yd in a steep, diving pass and after about three seconds observed many strikes. Since I was closing fast and approaching the airfield, which was beginning to throw up intense and accurate flak, I broke left and up, taking evasive action when about one-third of the way across the field. My wingman, who was behind me, saw the E/A touch ground, cartwheel and burn.

'During the above engagement my number three and four men had become separated from the flight, so my wingman and I set out on a course of 180 degrees at 5,000 ft in search of

Mustang IVs of No 26 Squadron, late 1945.

ground targets. Near Leipheim A/D we spotted an unidentified aircraft crossing the south-west corner of the field at 4,000 ft; 150 degrees. We increased our speed and closed on the E/A which we identified as an Me 262 with dark camouflage and large crosses on its wings. As I came in range, the jet made a sharp turn to the left, losing altitude. When I followed him, closing slowly, he started to let down his nosewheel, apparently intending to land. Closing further to 400 yd, I commenced firing. The first burst missed, but when the jet attempted to turn to the right I gave it to him again at about ten degrees deflection and observed many strikes. Large pieces of the E/A began to fly off and the fuselage exploded below the cockpit. The 262 then rolled to the right and went straight in from 800 ft, exploding as it went.'

RAF Mustang pilots also had encounters with enemy jet and rocket fighters in the closing stages of the war, as Captain D.H.

'Tom' Seaton recalls. In March 1945 Seaton, then a squadron leader, was commanding No 611 Squadron at Hunsford in Hertfordshire. No 611 Squadron had just re-equipped with P-51D Mustang IVs.

'I was posted to No 611 from 91 at Manston, and was informed that I would be responsible for re-equipping with Mustangs from the Spitfire IX which they then had. We were told to waste no time on this since there was an urgent requirement to provide more long range escort to Bomber Command and the Americans.

'We carried out several raids as fighter escort, usually high cover, and had a little luck, but there wasn't much fight left in the Luftwaffe at this stage of the war. The squadron claimed about six destroyed and several damaged, notably one Me 163 which had also finished off two Mustangs whose pilots became over-zealous and followed the 163 down until it hit the deck. Both Mustangs ran into intense flak and came close to following suit. However, luck prevailed and both pilots made emergency landings on the long runway at Manston, though neither Mustang ever flew again. In addition to the long-range escorting, we would fly to Schleswig-Holstein and cover the Me 262s on their airfields awaiting take-off to intercept our bombers. We made several hair-raising attacks on such targets, and Colonel Christie, our wing leader, was shot down on one such attack.

'There is no doubt that if we had had our Mustangs earlier in the war, we could have made a much greater contribution to defeating the Luftwaffe. The Spitfire was a great fighter with formidable firepower but did not adapt well to bigger and longer fuel tanks, whereas the Mustang had the fuel, albeit with a CG (centre of gravity) problem until the rear fuselage tank was empty and the wing tanks dropped. Of course, the six .5 guns were no replacement for the Spitfire's 20mm cannon, and the RR Merlin was essential to the fine

performance of the aircraft. However, even the Mustang sitting high above the bombers had little chance of catching an Me 262 that came into the attack 5–10,000 ft below. Fortunately there were not too many 262s and the *Luftwaffe* had a difficult time surviving on any airfield or autobahn in the face of the tremendous Allied air advantage. I have not mentioned ground attack; we were briefed by 12 Group on staying with the bombers and not leaving the vulnerable Lancasters open to Fw 190s and Me 262s on the return flight. Occasionally we would receive permission to detach a squadron to drop tanks and strafe anything in sight on the way home.'

Another pilot who flew long-range Mustang escort missions with No 611 Squadron was Flight Lieutenant James Grottick, who today is a Methodist minister in Warwick. Grottick had previously flown Tempest Vs with No 501 Squadron, also based at Hunsdon, on anti-V-1 patrols at

Mustang IVs of No 213 Squadron, RAF.

night, which was extremely dangerous work. At this stage of the war the flying bombs were being air-launched by Heinkel He 111s.

'Somewhere around the end of March 1945, word came through that all the V-1 sites had been overrun, and that our contribution was no longer required. Being still young, still madly in love with flying and probably a bit touched in the head, I viewed the possibility of no more ops with much dismay. But then I had a bright idea. On the other side of the Hunsdon airfield was No 611 Squadron. Its CO was Squadron Leader 'Tom' Seaton, who had been my flight commander when I first joined No 501 Squadron, and apart from flying together we had become good friends. So I hopped across to 611's dispersal, had a brief word in Tom Seaton's ear, and within an hour I was across on the strength of No 611 Squadron. To this day I am not at all sure that No 11 Group Fighter Command or anyone else knew about the transfer, but it was done.

'So it was that, with much relief, I found myself on Mustang IVs with the chance of starting a third tour of operations. With all the informality of the time I was shown over the cockpit of a Mustang. ("This, old boy is the fuel cock; this is the gun-button; this is the R/T button; that lever operates the flaps, and the brakes are operated by pressing the rudder pedals. Nothing to it, old boy. Just remember to have an extra ten knots on the approach for your girl friend, and ten knots for your mother-in-law, and the aircraft will virtually land itself.") That was about the sum total of my briefing/instruction on how to fly a P-51.

'Long-range Mustang escort operations were tests of endurance for the old "sit-upon". I recollect that the first op I did, no-one thought to tell me that you needed a water-cushion if you were to be seated immovable for four to five hours. I can still feel now the excruciating pain in my rear end after about two-and-a-half hours. On my third trip, heading somewhere into central Germany, my oxygen apparatus went on the blink. I owe my present ecclesiastical presence to the insistent voice of Tom Seaton, who recognized the signs of anoxia and bellowed at me to turn my oxygen on to emergency. Thereafter, for the next couple of hours or so, I had to fly with emergency oxygen for two minutes, then back to normal for a few minutes, then on to emergency again.

'Mostly, in those few operational trips, we were escorting high-level bombers (usually B-17s) on long-range missions to Munich and so on, or we were doing fighter protection patrols in, say, Denmark. The Mustang was a delightful aircraft, especially so with the Merlin engine. The cockpit (compared to a "Spit", say) was quite spacious, with a big bubble hood. In all a very nice aeroplane, and reasonably easy to bale out of!

'I managed seven pretty long-range operations before someone "got" me, somewhere south of Bremen in the Minden area on Sunday 21 April at 22,000 feet, maybe a bit lower. When I began to get a bit hot, and realised that all was not right, I made preparations to bale out. I remembered all that I had been told. Undo seat straps, undo R/T plug so that you don't hang yourself, release cockpit hood, onto your back and out you go. Alas, the first time I forgot that you needed to trim forward while holding the stick back, so that when inverted and you let go the stick, you are catapulted out. As it was, on the first attempt, when I let go the stick the nose fell, with the result that I just remained glued into my seat. The second attempt was much more successful and I went out like a pea out of a pod.'

Wesel was devastated by Allied bombing prior to the Rhine crossing. Mustangs formed a large proportion of the fighter escort.

James Grottick successfully evaded capture and made his way back to the Allied lines. In his absence, on 25 April, No 611 Squadron joined other Mustang units and the P-51s of the USAAF's 78th Fighter Group in escorting RAF Lancasters that were carrying out a heavy attack on Hitler's mountain retreat at Berchtesgaden. 'Tom' Seaton's log book records the occasion with the remark: 'The Alps most impressive today. Flak fair, Hitler's home a little bent!'

Meanwhile, in March 1945 enemy jet fighter activity had reached an unprecedented level, and this was to be sustained throughout most of April. In these two months, USAAF fighters alone reported 438 encounters, resulting in 280 combats with claims of forty-three Me 262s destroyed in the air, three probably destroyed and forty-five damaged, together with twenty-one destroyed and eleven damaged on the ground.

On 18 March, 1,250 USAAF bombers set course for Berlin to deliver the heaviest attack of the whole war on the German capital. A few miles short of the target the bombers were attacked by thirty-seven Me 262s of JG 7, which shot down nineteen bombers for the loss of two of their own number to defensive gunfire. The 262s fared worse on the following day. Five were shot down by the Mustang escorts, the 78th and 357th FGs claiming two each and the 359th one. On 20 March it was the 339th FG's turn to produce results, with three more Me 262s confirmed, but on the 21st the 78th FG claimed six, with two more the next day.

The Mustang pilots continued to score at a steady rate against the 262s into early April, but on the 4th the enemy jets repeated their earlier successes when forty-nine Me 262s of JG 7 attacked 150 B-17s over Nordhausen and destroyed fifteen of them. Four days later JG 7 – this time directing its attacks against the escorting American fighters – demonstrated the Me 262's enormous speed advantage by shooting down twenty-eight Mustangs, Lightnings and Thunderbolts in air battles that raged across central and northern Germany. Nevertheless, there was no escaping the fact that on this same day no fewer than 133 piston-engined Messer-schmitt 109s and Focke-Wulf 190s were destroyed by Allied fighters. No matter how many successes were registered by the German jets, they were too few and it was too late; the Allies remained firmly in control of the air. On 10 April, over a thousand American bombers launched massive attacks on the jet fighter bases of Oranienburg, Brandenburg-Briest, Parchim and Rechlin. The 262s shot down ten of the bombers, but with their bases devastated they were compelled to withdraw to air-fields as far away as Prague. The jet fighter units were broken up and scattered piece-meal, and in the final days their aircraft were grounded through lack of fuel.

Chapter 8
The China-Burma-India Theatre

On 4 July 1942, the China Air Task Force was activated in India as a unit of the Tenth Air Force. Command of the CATF devolved upon Brigadier-General Claire Chennault, who for several months had led the American Volunteer Group – the so-called 'Flying Tigers' – in action against the Japanese. With the activation of the CATF the AVG ceased to exist as an independent fighting unit, and few of its volunteer pilots, who had held the line for so long against impossible odds in Burma alongside the dwindling squadrons of the RAF, elected to remain in the theatre. Those who did provided a nucleus of experienced pilots for the newly-activated 23rd Fighter Group, which absorbed the resources of the AVG. The latter amounted to a handful of war-weary Curtiss P-40s and Republic P-43s. The resources of the Tenth Air Force, which was little more than a paper command at this stage, were

even more slender: eight bombers and ten fighters.

Shortly after assuming command of the China Air Task Force, Chennault submitted a memorandum to Lieutenant-General Joseph Stillwell, Commander-in-Chief of the American forces in the CBI theatre, outlining his views on the potential of China-based air power. His objectives for the CATF were to protect the air supply route over the 'Hump' between India and China; to destroy Japanese aircraft in China in large numbers; to damage and destroy Japanese military bases in China and encourage Chinese resistance; to disrupt Japanese shipping on the Yangtze and Yellow Rivers and along the China coast; to damage Japanese bases in Thailand, Indo-China, Burma and Formosa and interdict Japanese air concentrations being ferried from Chinese bases across Indo-China and Thailand to Burma; and to undermine the efficiency and morale of the Japanese Air

Wreck of a 23rd FG P-51, destroyed by the retreating US forces at Nanking, China.

Line-up of P-51Ds awaiting delivery to the Pacific Theatre of Operations.

Force by achieving these objectives, Chennault asked Stillwell for 100 P-51 fighters and thirty B-25 bombers. He also requested operational independence from the Tenth Air Force command in Delhi.

Material reinforcements such as these were vital, for the activation of the CATF did not result in any immediate improvement in the material situation of what had been the AVG. The CATF inherited fifty-seven aircraft (fifty-four P-40s and three P-43s) from the AVG, of which only forty were airworthy, together with seven airworthy B-25s from the Tenth Air Force. With a total of forty-seven operational aircraft, short of spares and fuel, the CATF faced a formidable enemy along a 2,000-mile front stretching from Honkew to Hong Kong and Burma to Indo-China. In terms of air strength, the CATF was outnumbered by eight to one.

Despite the shortcomings the CATF carried out a number of very successful offensive operations during the latter months of 1942, the B-25s being supplemented by B-24s on temporary deployment from India, but as the new year approached shortages of fuel and spare parts forced the curtailment of all CATF activities. During the early months of 1943 the supply problem became so acute that the CATF lacked sufficient fuel to engage in any offensive operations. Blaming the shortages of fuel and supplies on the Tenth Air Force, Chennault proceeded with his plan to create an air force in China independent of the Delhi command; he secured the support of President Roosevelt, who decided to overrule his military advisors and announced his intention of placing Chennault in command of a new air unit in China and of building this unit up to a strength of 500 aircraft a soon as conditions permitted.

In March 1943 the China Air Task Force ceased to exist and the Fourteenth Air Force was activated, with Chennault as Commander-in-Chief with the rank of major-general. In April, Chennault put forward new operational plans; he proposed to take advantage of good flying weather to launch a sustained two-month offensive against the Japanese in July 1942 with the aim of wresting air superiority from them over China. In August, after this initial objective had been achieved, he proposed to move his medium bombers to forward bases in eastern China from which they would launch a major campaign against Japanese shipping along the Yangtze and the Haiphong, Hainan and the coastal ports. During September 1943, the Fourteenth Air Force would widen its activities to include Japanese shipping in the Formosa Straits and the entire Indo-China coast, following which the bombers would move eastward, attacking Formosa and the Shanghai-Nanking-Hankow triangle. By the end of the year the Fourteenth Air Force would be ready to move against the Japanese Home Islands.

To accomplish these goals successfully, Chennault outlined his minimum requirement to Roosevelt. He would need seventy-four P-40s, seventy-five P-51s, thirty-five B-24s, forty-eight B-25s and a photo-reconnaissance force, probably a mixture of F-5 Lightnings and F-6 Mustangs. The first fighter reinforcement arrived in April 1943, in the shape of P-40s, and were followed in May by thirty-five B-24s of the 308th Bombardment Group; with the arrival of the latter the Fourteenth Air Force had the capacity to strike against all Japanese installations in China, Indo-China, Burma and Thailand.

With these resources Chennault was able to implement his planned offensive, beginning with an assault on Japanese shipping, but as yet he did not have enough fighters to establish air superiority and, when the B-24s attacked targets that were beyond the range of the P-40s, the bombers suffered heavy losses. On 14 August, when fourteen B-24s attacked Haiphong without fighter escort, two were destroyed and ten more severely damaged, and a week later five more bombers were shot down in an unescorted raid on Hankow.

A Mustang lines up for take-off on a bomber escort mission in the Pacific.

Matters improved in September with the arrival of the first Allison-engined P-51A Mustangs and also some P-38 Lightnings, which were able to accompany the bombers on long-range missions. On 25 November, eight P-51s and eight P-38s accompanied fourteen B-25s in a spectacularly successful attack on Shinchiku airfield, Formosa, where Fourteenth Air Force reconnaissance aircraft had detected seventy-five enemy fighters and bombers the day before. Flying at low altitude across the Formosa Strait to avoid radar detection, the Americans, joined by Chinese-manned B-25s of the Chinese-American Composite Wing, achieved complete surprise and destroyed forty-two enemy aircraft on the ground in less than fifteen minutes for no loss to themselves.

In the Fourteenth Air Force, the P-51s were assigned to the 23rd Fighter Group (74th, 75th and 76th Fighter Squadrons). Meanwhile, the Tenth Air Force, operating against the Japanese in Assam, had also begun to receive Mustangs in the late summer of 1943; these, a mixture of P-51As and A-36s, were assigned to the 311th Fighter-Bomber Group (528th, 529th and 530th Fighter Squadrons) which, together with the P-40-equipped 80th Fighter Group, provided support for deep-penetration ground forces such as Merrill's Marauders.

In October 1943, the American-controlled Northern Combat Area Command, with two Chinese armies raised and maintained from US sources, began an advance in the Hukawng Valley with the eventual object of capturing the airstrip and strategic town of Myitkyina. It was anticipated that the advance would produce heavy demands on the Tenth Air Force for close support, and since neither the 80th nor the 311th Fighter Groups had any experience in this kind of work, detailed preparations were made to ensure close air-ground co-operation. The first move was to establish an air-ground support radio team in the 1st Tactical Communication Squadron to receive all requests for air-ground support, to screen these requests and eliminate those not suitable for air attack, and to convey accepted requirements to air headquarters together with all information necessary for the execution of the mission.

In the advance towards Myitkyina, it had been agreed at first that troops asking for air support would lay out a panel at a specified distance from the target and pointing towards it. However, when the deep jungle made it difficult to place such a signal and even more difficult for the pilots to spot it, smoke shells were mortared on to the target according to a prearranged code, so that their bursts formed, for example, a triangle or a rectangle. This method was also unsatisfactory because the signal

pattern was frequently blurred by drift or other causes, including diversionary smoke shells fired by the enemy.

A more satisfactory device was the use of coordinates superimposed on special photographs of enemy-held areas. A transparent grid of plastic made it possible to divide any print into twenty-four squares with the usual horizontal and vertical designations by number and letter. With copies of the appropriate print in the hands of all interested units and headquarters, air and ground, it required only the specification of the coordinates to pinpoint the desired target. Much vital photographic work in connection with this was carried out by the 8th Photo Reconnaissance Group, which was activated on 1 October 1943 and was equipped with F-5, F-6 and F-7 aircraft. During the long and arduous campaign its aircraft undertook many hundreds of photo and visual reconnaissance missions over Burma, China, French Indo-China and Thailand, as well as bombing and strafing enemy installations and carrying out bomber escorts. A detachment of the 8th PRG was placed at the disposal of air headquarters in November 1943 to assure rapid coverage of target areas.

The highest efficiency in close support was achieved by combining the use of coordinates with ground-controlled radio guidance. With both the target and friendly troops located by grid, the pilot reached his destination at a pre-arranged time and made radio contact with the air-ground liaison party. A dry run over the target provided a further check, so that errors in flight could be detected and corrected before the actual bombing was undertaken. The A-36 and P-51 pilots, with the advantage of a highly stable bombing platform that resulted in high precision, became adept at seeking out and destroying the most elaborately hidden Japanese artillery positions, dug-in machine guns, slit trenches, road blocks or troop concentrations. Errors became increasingly few and a spirit of camaraderie

'Jumpin' Jacques', a 3rd Air Commando Group P-51D. Note the Bugs Bunny motif.

seldom encountered elsewhere grew up between the air and ground personnel.

By May 1944 airstrips had been built along the Hukawng and Mogaung valleys that were suitable for use by fighters and transport aircraft. The 88th Fighter Squadron, equipped with P-40s, was based at Shingbwiyang; the 528th Fighter Squadron, with a mixture of P-51s and A-36s, was located at Tingkawk Sakan, alongside a flight of P-40s of the 20th Tactical Reconnaissance Squadron. The 311th Fighter Group's other two squadrons, the 529th and 530th, remained in Assam with two squadrons of P-40s.

As the siege of Myitkyina began, it was decided to base a flight of eight P-40s on the newly captured west strip so that aircraft would be immediately available for close support operations. These aircraft – the number was later raised to twelve – operated from a base that was probably closer to enemy lines than any other in the history of air warfare, for Japanese machine-guns were only 1,000 yards away and aircraft came under fire every time they took off and landed. Although the first line of enemy emplacements was soon destroyed by dive-bombing attacks, carried out by the P-40s and by flights of A-36s that were deployed there periodically from the 528th Fighter Squadron, other machine guns a short distance to the rear remained a constant threat. A detachment of three P-40s of the 20th Tactical Reconnaissance Squadron was also ordered to Myitkyina

A 21st FG P-51D comes to grief after suffering an engine failure.

together with a small processing laboratory, which could produce prints of target areas with the minimum loss of time.

In the weeks that followed the opening of the siege, it was the P-40s based at the Myitkyina strip that carried out most of the missions directed against the town and its immediate defences, the pilots becoming so proficient that they were called upon even when friendly forces were within seventy-five yards of the target. P-51s and A-6s were also called in from Tingkawk Sakan and the Assam strips for less exacting tasks; since most of these pilots were not as familiar with the sector as those based on the west strip, they relied on radio direction for locating the target. They normally did not land at Myitkyina, but made their approaches over the strip for any last-minute instructions from the local ground-air liaison station.

The intensity of the air support effort at Myitkyina was remarkable. At the height of the siege the P-40 and Mustang pilots were flying as many as six sorties each, and it was by no means unusual for a flight of four aircraft to accomplish twenty sorties within twenty-four hours. In all, the fighter-bombers flew 2,515 sorties between 17 May 1944, when the siege began, and 3 August, when the town fell. This was an average of thirty-three sorties a day, and it was accomplished during the monsoon season, when breaks in the weather were few. The monsoon caused particular problems for the P-51 pilots of the 528th Fighter Squadron; although their strip at Tingkawk Sakan was only twenty minutes' flying time away, they frequently found that the weather had clamped down by the time they reached the target area.

Normally, the fighter-bombers engaged in close support at Myitkyina carried 250 lb bombs, fused for one-tenth of a second delay to permit penetration and narrow the area of the explosion. The pilots dived on the target at an angle of forty-five degrees, starting at 5,000 feet and pulling up at 1,000 feet, sighting between the second and third wing guns so that they could detect even the slightest deviation. Using this technique, bomb strikes within fifteen yards of the target were normal.

The capture of Myitkyina, which was very much a joint effort between Stillwell's Chinese divisions, Merrill's Maurauders and the British Chindit Brigade, coupled with the decisive battles at Imphal and Kohima, effectively marked the destruction of Japanese power in northern Burma and opened the way for the Allied reconquest of the country.

Late in August 1944, with Stillwell's forces engaged in mopping-up operations in northern Burma, the 311th Fighter Group was transferred to China, where the Fourteenth Air Force was under very heavy pressure. In April – mainly in response to the Fourteenth Air Force's strategic bombing offensive – the Japanese had launched their last major offensive of the war, Operation *Ichi-Go*, and had succeeded in clearing part of Honan Province that had been in Chinese Government (Kuomintang) hands since 1938. Once this was secured, the main Japanese offensive began on 27 May, and over the next six months various converging Japanese drives slowly resulted in the linking up of their existing holdings. By late November 1944, the Japanese were able to claim the establishment of uninterrupted overland communications between Singapore and Manchuria. To some extent the Japanese gains were illusory, for they left their forces badly over-extended and by this time the decision had been made to use the Marianas, instead of China, as the main base for the strategic air offensive against Japan, but it was nevertheless a dangerous period.

In fact, using south-west China as a base for striking at the Japanese home Islands with the new Boeing B-29 Superfortress bombers had never been a particularly realistic option for the Americans. Construction of the necessary airfields in itself presented enormous problems; for a start the only road linking Allied territory with China ran through Burma, and early

Firemen put out the flames following a taxying accident to a P-51D of the 15th FG.

in 1944 this had been severed by the Japanese advance. All supplies and equipment therefore had to be flown into China from airfields in India or Assam, often through treacherous weather over the 'Hump'. As if the climatic problems were not enough, the meagre trickle of supplies that did get through had to be shared between Chennault's Fourteenth Air Force, the Chinese and the XX Bomber Command, the latter newly activated to prosecute the strategic air offensive. All this led to considerable bickering between the respective commanders, each of whom was inclined to believe that the others were receiving more than a fair slice of the cake. The XX Bomber Command, as a newly established organization requiring large quantities of bombs, fuel and spare parts, had to fight hard for its existence during its early days.

Despite all the difficulties, however, the Command became operational during June 1944, and on the 15th of that month B-29s carried out their first attack on the Japanese

mainland. More raids from Chinese territory were carried out during the weeks that followed, but although the XX Bomber Command's commander, General Curtis LeMay, made superhuman efforts to raise the standards of operational efficiency, the B-29s were able to average only two sorties a month, and some of these were directed against targets in Thailand and Malaya. In all, XX Bomber Command dropped only 800 tons of bombs on Japanese targets while operating from Chinese bases, and it became increasingly clear that strategic operations against Japan would never be fully effective until bases in the South-West Pacific became available. Also, bomber operations from such bases would have the advantage of long-range fighter escort.

In November 1944 the Fourteenth Air Force consisted of thirty-six combat squadrons, grouped under the 68th and 69th Composite Wings, the Chinese-American Composite Wing, and the 312th Fighter Wing. The fighter element of the 69th Composite Wing was the 51st Fighter

Group which had begun re-equipping with P-51B/C Mustangs in April 1944. The 51st's component units were the 16th, 25th, 26th and 449th Fighter Squadrons. With its headquarters at Kunming, the 69th Wing's task was the defence of the Hump route and south-west China.

The 68th Composite Wing comprised the 23rd Fighter Group and the 118th Tactical Reconnaissance Squadron, which had also begun to receive P-51B/Cs in the spring of 1944. Its principal task was to support the Chinese ground forces along the Hankow-Canton railway, interdicting enemy lines of communication in south and south-east China and maintaining a counter-air campaign. The Chinese-American Composite Wing, whose fighter elements (the 3rd and 5th Fighter Groups) were mostly equipped with P-40s, had its combat area in central China, in particular the regions south of the Yellow River and as far east as the Nanking-Shanghai area. The 312th Fighter Wing, comprising the P-51B/C Mustangs of the 311th Fighter Group and the P-47s of the 81st Fighter Group (91st and 92nd Fighter Squadrons) had once been restricted to the defence of the airfields in the Chengtu area, but by the end of 1944 its mission was defined as the interdiction of the Tungpu, Ping-Han, Tsingpu and Suiyuan-Peking railways. To carry out this mission more effectively the 490th Bombardment Squadron (Medium) was also placed under the operational control of the 312th Wing, and in February 1945 three squadrons of B-24s were assigned to it.

The 69th Composite Wing was somewhat divorced from the crucial operations in China during the last two months of 1944 and the first six months of 1945, as its primary mission was in French Indo-China and part of Kwangsi Province. As part of its additional task of defending the Hump route, the Wing also supported the British in the last phases of the Salweek campaign and the reoccupation of central Burma, deploying its Mustangs for operations from the Salweek bases. Having bombed their assigned targets, the Mustangs went on to Tingkawk Sakan, where they re-armed and took off to bomb another target in central

A ground crew member waves a P-51D from the flight path prior to an escort mission over the Pacific.

20th Air Force P-51Ds with long-range 'Tokyo tanks'.

Burma on the return flight to China. After the reoccupation of central Burma, the 69th Wing's Mustangs carried out interdiction missions in Indo-China, giving much support to units of the French Foreign Legion and Viet Minh guerrillas who were fighting the Japanese on the border with Yunnan Province. Ironically, the Viet Minh were led by one Ho Chi Minh, who was to cause the Americans a great deal of trouble in later years.

Although the Fourteenth Air Force was stronger than ever before, with fighter sorties reaching a new peak in the last three months of 1944 (4,054 in October, 3,288 in November and 3,278 in December) the Americans were fighting at a great disadvantage. Not only had the Japanese extended their corridor southward from Hankow, overrunning four airfields, but they had also surrounded and besieged half a dozen more easterly airstrips. Within that area, 150,000 poorly-equipped Chinese troops were still fighting, and in desperate need of continual air support.

To this end, in November, General Chennault set up the East China Air Task Force. Under a plan designated *Strongpoint*, he divided the 68th Composite Wing into two forces, the 23rd Group's 75th and 76th Fighter Squadrons remaining west of the corridor while the 74th Fighter Squadron and the 118th Tactical Reconnaissance Squadron were located east of it. The latter two squadrons were strengthened by a detachment of Liberators from the 308th Bombardment Group.

On 19 November 1944 two of these aircraft, operating from Suichwan, carried out a reconnaissance that revealed large enemy troop concentrations eighty-five miles to the north-west, a move that suggested the Japanese were planning to overrun the remaining eastern airfields before turning towards Kunming and the airstrips in that area. The Japanese struck on 15 January 1945 and the Chinese forces were soon in retreat, although still in fighting trim. For the first few days of the battle the 23rd Fighter Group's pilots, taking advantage of good weather, repeatedly bombed and strafed the advancing enemy and restricted them to movement by night. Then bad weather set in, curtailing operations, and on 27 January the 23rd FG and its associated units were forced into a hasty evacuation of Suichwan when the strip was threatened by the Japanese. By mid-February the only field left east of the corridor was Changting.

Despite this setback, the East China Air Task Force made a valiant effort. Although the Japanese were known to have overwhelming material air superiority – as many as 160 bombers and 400 fighters – the Japanese Army Air Force had remained surprisingly inactive. Its lack of an adequate early warning system had enabled the Mustang pilots to carry out many successful strafing attacks on enemy airfields, where they had found aircraft parked wingtip to wingtip with no attempt at dispersal. The Mustangs usually attacked in two waves; one would strafe while the other provided top cover, and then the two would change places. In all, the 74th FS and the 118th TRS flew 747 sorties, dropping 110 tons of bombs. The East China Air Task

Force claimed 312 enemy aircraft destroyed, mostly on the ground; the Americans lost no Mustangs in air combat, but fifteen were shot down by ground fire and thirteen were lost through other causes.

The principal Japanese Army Air Force fighter encountered by the Americans and their allies in the CBI was the Nakajima Ki-43 *Hayabusa* (Oscar), but as the war progressed numbers of Nakajima Ki-44 *Shoki* (Tojo) fighters also began to appear. Neither was a match for the Merlin-engined Mustang, and in general the JAAF pilots were of inferior calibre to their counterparts in the Imperial Japanese Navy, who had the benefit of far better equipment in the shape of the Mitsubishi A6M5 Zero and, later, the J2M3 *Raiden* (Jack). Some of the American pilot achieved respectable scores in air combat; one was Lt Col Edward McComas, whose most fruitful day was 23 December 1944, when he destroyed five enemy fighters in the

A 21st FG P-51D, after suffering a tyre burst on Iwo Jima, April 1945.

space of an hour. While leading sixteen Mustangs of the 118th Tactical Reconnaissance Squadron back from an attack on the Wuchang-Hankow ferry terminals, he strafed the Japanese airfield at Wuchang, destroying two aircraft on the ground. As he climbed away, he sighted an Oscar fighter and attacked it from astern, seeing its pilot bale out. Another enemy airfield Ehur Tao Kow, lay on his route home and he decided to attack it too. Arriving overhead, he sighted a pair of Oscars taking off and dived on them just as they became airborne. He fired on the leading aircraft and it rolled sharply, colliding with the second fighter. Both Oscars crashed in flames on the airfield boundary. Pulling his Mustang round in a tight turn he came in behind two more Oscars and shot both of them down.

The top scores understandably went to the pilots of the 23rd Fighter Group, which was in action in the CBI longer than any other unit. Captain John F. Hampshire of the 23rd also shot down fourteen enemy aircraft before his death in action in February 1943, before the Group equipped with Mustangs. The group's top-scoring Mustang pilot was Colonel John Herbst, known as 'Pappy' among his pilots because at thirty-five he was a good ten years older than most of them. On 1 January 1945 Herbst's score stood at fifteen enemy aircraft destroyed. Then, on the 16th, he shot down two Japanese bombers and on the following day he destroyed a Tojo fighter over Tachang, bringing his score up to eighteen.

The counter-air measures by the East China Air Task Force, while serving the immediate end of protecting the Chinese ground forces from interference by the JAAF, were also part of a general effort by the Fourteenth Air Force to keep the enemy air force pinned down throughout China. It was hoped that the attempt to gain complete air supremacy would contribute towards holding the Japanese armies within their established lines, and also contribute to the Allied effort in the Pacific,

which by this time had extended as far as the Philippine Islands. All of Chennault's command in some measure shared in the offensive, but the 312th Fighter Wing, now free of the responsibility of defending the B-29 bases at Chengtu, played an especially active part. Situated west of the corridor at Sian, under the command of Brig Gen Russell E. Randall, the 312th's Mustangs attacked numerous enemy airfields between November 1944 and the end of February 1945. Again, most of the Mustang losses sustained during this phase were the result of ground fire; whether because the better trained and better equipped enemy units were committed to the hard fighting in the Pacific or for some other reason, Japanese reaction in the air was largely confined to night attacks, never in great strength, against Allied airfields within the east China pocket. The bombing destroyed six Mustangs, three B-24 tankers and 4,000 gallons of aviation fuel, a serious loss in view of the supply situation.

By mid-February 1945, the counter-air programme had succeeded so well that the Fourteenth Air Force turned much of its effort to interdiction. The purpose was to cut down the supplies reaching the Japanese Army, to disrupt its administration of the conquered provinces, and to prevent the development of effective overland communications with the southern parts of the Empire. While Thunderbolts struck bridges along the southern Tungpu and attacked railroads and highways, Mustangs hit the Ping-Han bridges and, their range extended by wing tanks, strafed locomotives along the Tsingpu. Within a month, intelligence reported that 142 locomotives had been destroyed and thirty-seven bridges rendered temporarily unserviceable. Intelligence also indicated that damaged locomotives had been hauled into northern China for repair, and accordingly three squadrons of Liberators of the 308th Bombardment Group were taken off coastal sweeps and placed under the operational control of the 312th Wing for strikes against

20th AF P-51Ds on patrol. Note the Japanese 'kill' markings under the leading aircraft's cockpit.

the repair centres. On 9 March 1945 thirty-one Liberators, escorted by twelve Mustangs of the 311th Fighter Group, caused considerable damage to the repair shops at Sinsiang. On 23 March twenty-eight Liberators, escorted by sixteen Mustangs, attacked the Tsinan yards and a Yellow River bridge which carried an average daily traffic of 3,000 tons; the yards and shops were destroyed and the bridge severely damaged.

In April, the heavy bombers of the 308th Bomber Group were transferred to India for supply operations over the Hump, and it became necessary to restrict fighter attacks in order to conserve fuel. Accordingly, the Fourteenth Air Force drew up a revised target list of bridges within the assigned area of responsibility of each fighter wing and gave orders to keep a definite number impassable at all times. In general, the fighters of the 312th Fighter Wing, the Chinese-American Composite

Wing and the 68th Composite Wing were used against the bridges, while medium bombers were used for attacks on marshalling yards, locomotive repair facilities and other strongly built structures. The 51st Fighter Group and the 341st Bombardment Group performed similar tasks in Indo-China, where by the end of May the damage inflicted was heavy enough to interrupt permanently the traffic from Vinh to the China border. By June, with three bridges unusable within a distance of forty miles, the Japanese abandoned rail transportation and were forced to rely entirely on motor vehicles.

Despite supply difficulties and the loss of the east China airfields, the Fourteenth Air Force continued to press the enemy hard, and targets along the Yangtze River received such close attention that on 21 March 1945 the Japanese struck south-west from Lushan in a bid to overrun the northern airfields. At the same time, a column swept north along the Han River valley to provide a pincer movement against Laohokow. Lacking air cover, the enemy columns moved by night against only slight resistance by the defending Chinese ground forces. On 25 March the installations at Laohokow were destroyed by the Americans and all personnel evacuated. Sian and Ankang were next in line for Japanese occupation, but Chinese resistance stiffened into a stubborn defence and the Fourteenth Air Force provided excellent support. Mustangs and Thunderbolts from Sian and Ankang struck repeatedly against the bridges and concentration points along the enemy's line of march and patrolled Japanese road and river lines of communication. The 312th Fighter Wing concentrated its attacks north of the Yellow River, while the Chinese-American Composite Wing struck on the south. The 311th Fighter Group, the 81st

Fighter Group, the 426th Night Fighter Squadron (equipped with Northrop P-61 Black Widows) and CACW's 3rd Fighter Group and 1st and 2nd Bombardment Squadrons made a maximum effort. During April ground controllers directed the pilots to their targets as the enemy took refuge in caves, foxholes and bunkers in the hills and villages, and the Japanese attempt to capture more Fourteenth Air Force airfields was smashed for good.

The Japanese Army in China, however, was far from exhausted. In order to break the supply bottleneck the Japanese launched a second offensive against the Fourteenth Air Force on 10 April 1945. Concentrating their attack against the American airfields at Chihchiang, the Japanese hoped to neutralize the Fourteenth Air Force in central China, gain control of the vital Hsiang valley, the gateway to Chungking and Kunming, and

The pilot was lucky to walk away from this 506th FG P-51D after struggling home to a belly landing on Iwo Jima. Both wings sheared off and the fuel tanks exploded.

compel the Fourteenth Air Force to interrupt its interdiction campaign. To accomplish these goals, the Japanese massed an army of some 60,000 men and a small air unit of several fighter squadrons.

Japanese preparations for the offensive were detected by air reconnaissance, giving the Chinese and Americans time to prepare their defences. Chinese forces in the area of the Chihchiang bases numbered about 100,000 men, giving the Allies an almost two to one advantage in manpower. In the past such numerical advantages had meant little to the Chinese in the light of the superior equipment, training and morale of their adversaries, but now the situation was different. Tactical air power had decimated the Japanese air strength in China, and the enemy were confronting Chinese armies in the Hsiang valley which were comparatively well equipped and supplied.

Co-operating closely with the Fourteenth Air Force, the Chinese succeeded in repulsing the Japanese attack in one of the first truly co-ordinated air-to-ground

actions of the war in China. For two months, the Chinese and Americans, co-ordinating their efforts through air-ground liaison teams, held the Japanese in check. While the Chinese held the Japanese on the ground, Fourteenth Air Force Mustangs, Thunderbolts, P-40s and medium bombers attacked them with napalm, anti-personnel bombs and fired millions of rounds of ammunition. As the Allies had total air superiority there was little the Japanese could do to protect themselves, and as a consequence they suffered heavy casualties.

The Japanese offensive petered out in June 1945, after they had suffered a decisive defeat at Chihchiang. The effects of the Chinese-American victory were immediate, the Japanese being forced to retreat from east China and the Yangtse. After seven years of war, victory was in sight. It was a victory in which the Mustang's ground-attack capability had played an enormous part, and it was to have a parallel five years later, in Korea.

Chapter 9
Mustang Operations in the Pacific Theatre

THE FIRST Mustang variant to see service in the Pacific Theatre was the F-6D reconnaissance version, which began to replace the Curtiss P-40s of the 82nd Tactical Reconnaissance Squadron at Morotai in November 1944. The 82nd TRS therefore became the original Mustang unit in the South-West Pacific Area. Plans were also made to allocate the type to the 110th TRS at the same time, but because this squadron's TacR P-40s were heavily involved in support of the fighting at Leyte and Mindoro in the Philippines conversion was delayed, and it was not until February 1945 that the 110th TRS began to receive its F-6Ds.

Early in 1945 two Fifth Air Force fighter groups operating in the South-West Pacific Area were re-equipped with P-51D Mustangs. The 348th Fighting Group began exchanging its P-47s for Mustangs squadron for squadron, completing the conversion late in March. Beginning in January, the plan had been to allow each

A P-51D approaching to land at Iwo Jima.

squadron twenty to thirty days' training with the new aircraft, but operational commitments in the Philippines reduced this training period to about a week for each squadron. The 35th FG also received its first P-51s early in March, and all three of its squadrons had checked out by the end of the month. Many pilots were reluctant to part with the 'Jug', as the P-47 was affectionately known, but its weight required long runways and this involved delays in positioning it forward to support the rapid advances being made by the ground forces. The P-47 nevertheless remained operational in the SWPA until the end of the war with the 58th Fighter Group.

Another unit to use the P-51D in the SWPA early in 1943 was the 3rd Air Commando Group, which moved to the Philippines in December and was assigned to the Fifth Air Force for operations with P-51, C-47 and L-5 aircraft. It operated in support of ground forces on Luzon and also provided escorts at a later date for missions to Formosa and the China coast, as well as providing top cover for convoys.

In the Pacific Operational Area (POA), the province of the Seventh and Twentieth Air Forces, the first unit to re-equip with the Mustang was the 15th Fighter Group, comprising the 4th, 47th and 48th Fighter Squadrons. The group was assigned to the Seventh Air Force and initially remained part of the Hawaiian air defence system, detaching aircraft at times for operations against the Japanese in the central and south Pacific. While undergoing training for very long-range escort missions, the 21st Fighter Group, (46th, 72nd and 73rd FS) which also formed part of the Hawaiian air defences, also re-equipped with P-51Ds in February 1945, both groups having previously operated P-39s and later P-38s.

At the end of December 1944 only ninety-five P-51s had been assigned to the Far East Air Forces' first-line strength, and this figure included aircraft on route to the theatre from the USA. High operational losses in the campaigns for Leyte and Mindoro meant that FEAF was running close to the danger line in terms of replacement aircraft, and in a letter to General H. H. Arnold, the Commanding General, US Army Air Forces, FEAF's commander General George Kenney expressed concern about his lack of single-engined fighters. The Army Air Force had cut back P-47 deliveries, and P-51s were not arriving in sufficient numbers to replace losses and meet conversion requirements. Kenney received an assurance, among others, that P-51 groups would be fully equipped by late February. He also requested and received forty-seven late-model P-38 Lightnings released by the Seventh Air Force on its conversion to P-51s, so that the threatened shortfall in fighter strength was curtailed before it became critical. While P-51s remained in short supply, Kenney agreed to retain the 58th Fighter Group as a Thunderbolt unit, at least until he could evaluate the combat suitability of the new P-47Ns offered him as replacements.

Both types were soon to prove their worth in the battle for Iwo Jima. The decision to capture the island had been taken as early as July 1944, at a time when strategic attacks by long-range B-29s on the Japanese Home Islands were about to begin. On 14 July 1944 General Arnold had sent a memorandum to the Joint Planning Staff drawing attention to the Nakajima Ki-84, a new and heavily armed fighter with which the Japanese might be able to inflict prohibitive losses on the B-29s. To provide escort for the bombers, he recommended the seizure of Iwo Jima, which was within Mustang combat radius of Tokyo, and approved a plan for assigning five groups of P-51s and P-47Ns to XXI Bomber Command for escort duties. It was also assumed that these fighters might conduct offensive sweeps over Japan as well as provide fighter escort. Moreover, Arnold reasoned that if Iwo Jima's airfields had their runways extended to very heavy bomber specifications, they could serve as

Servicing a Mustang on Iwo Jima. Engines were badly affected by volcanic dust.

emergency landing grounds or staging bases for the B-29s.

Planning for the seizure of Iwo Jima (Operation *Detachment*) began at once. The operational plan, which was changed a number of times but was more or less finalized by December 1944, envisaged a brief and bloody battle lasting three or four days. (In fact, it was to last a month). Plans called for the early development of three airfields, to be operational by D plus seven, D plus ten and D plus fifty respectively. As soon as possible after the assault the responsibility for the defence of the island was to pass from the Navy to the Air Defense Command, to be headed by Brig Gen Ernest Moore of VII Fighter Command. He was to have a sizeable fighter force comprising 222 P-51Ds of the 15th and

21st Fighter Groups, twenty-four P-61D Black Widows of the 548th and 549th Night Fighter Squadrons, and – at a later date – 111 P-47Ns of the 306th Fighter Group.

The assault on Iwo Jima by US Marines began on 19 February 1945, and by the 25th the seaborne troops of V Amphibious Corps were firmly established ashore. Fierce fighting for possession of the island was still in progress when the Mustangs of the 15th Fighter Group began arriving at Iwo's South Field on 6 March. The P-51s flew their first mission two days later, and on 10 March, the day the escort carriers with their naval fighter squadrons left the area, the 15th FG maintained constant patrols with flights of eight Mustangs between 0700 and 1830 hrs. At the request of ground commanders they strafed and bombed enemy pillboxes, cave entrances, gun emplacements, slit trenches, troops and stores, flying 125 sorties in the course of the day. Although the group's pilots were inexperienced in close support they learned quickly, pressing home their strikes at minimum altitudes and earning considerable praise from the ground troops.

The 15th Fighter Group also provided daylight combat air patrol, putting up dawn and dusk flights of twelve P-51s from 7 to 11 March, after which the patrols were reduced to eight aircraft. At night, two P-61s of the 548th NFS took over. This routine remained virtually unchanged until the end of the war, although the task was more widely distributed as more units arrived: the 549th Night Fighter Squadron on 20 March, the 21st Fighter Group on 23rd March, and the 306th Fighter Group on 11 May.

The Mustangs also took over the task of neutralizing the neighbouring islands of Chichi Jima and Haha Jima, previously targets for B-24s and carrier aircraft. The first strike was made on 11 March when the hard-pressed 15th FG, its airfield still under occasional enemy artillery fire, sent out

GIs watch as a P-51 flies overhead. Conditions on Iwo were rough for all personnel.

sixteen P-51s. With General Moore flying as an observer, the formation dropped eight tons of bombs between Susaki airfield and Futami Ko on Chichi Jima. Daily strikes on these targets by a similar number of Mustangs continued throughout March. Priority targets were operational aircraft, shipping, Susaki airfield and other military installations, but since enemy aircraft and shipping were seldom found the airfield itself took the main weight of the attacks. Only two Mustangs were lost to enemy action, and eight through other causes. Inadequate photographic coverage made target selection difficult, and in fact there was very little on the islands to hit, but the sorties denied the enemy effective use of the airfields and harbours and provided valuable experience of over-water flying for the Mustang pilots, experience that would stand them in good stead on future long-range missions to Japan.

B-29 night-bombing operations against Japan had been in progress for some time, but with Iwo Jima safely in American hands and long-range fighter escort available, XXI Bomber Command could now alternate its policy of night area bombing attacks with one of daylight precision attacks on industrial targets, with priority assigned to aero-engine plants. The first of these missions, against the Nakajima-Musashi factory, was flown on 7 April 1945, with 108 Mustangs of VII Fighter Command from Iwo Jima escorting B-29s of the 73rd Bombardment Wing. On this and subsequent missions to Japan each P-51D carried a 165 US-gallon drop tank on each wing shackle. The raid of 7 April was the first time that US land-based fighters had flown over the Japanese home islands. On this occasion, enemy fighter opposition was slight and was easily beaten off.

The strategic bombing campaign against Japan did not proceed without interruption. On 1 April 1945 US forces went ashore on Okinawa, the largest of the Ryuku chain of islands lying only 500 miles off the Japanese mainland. By 4 April 60,000 troops had been landed, but although the landings themselves were accomplished with relative ease the Americans soon found themselves involved in what was to become one of the fiercest battles of the war. The Japanese resisted fanatically with every means at their disposal, including swarms of Kamikaze suicide aircraft. In all, 1,900 Kamikaze attacks were made on the Allied fleet off the island. The suicide pilots scored 182 direct hits, sinking twenty-five ships and damaging many more. The situation became so critical that all available air units, including XXI Bomber Command, had to be sent to the assistance of the invasion force.

Between 17 April and 11 May, attacks were carried out on seventeen Kamikaze bases by the B-29s and also by the Mustangs of VII Fighter Command. All the enemy airfields were on the southern Japanese islands of Shikoku and Kyushu. On these strafing attacks the Mustangs carried six HVAR (High Velocity Aircraft Rockets) in addition to their long-range tanks, which raised the gross weight of the aircraft well above the normal maximum of 12,100 lb and often made take-offs from Iwo Jima's runways, which was always accomplished amid clouds of volcanic dust, a tricky business. This three-week series of strikes produced rather disappointing results, for although Kamikaze operations were hampered by the attacks on the enemy bases they continued to present a serious threat to the Allied task forces.

On 14 May XXI Bomber Command returned to strategic operations and put up 472 B-29s for a daylight incendiary attack on Nagoya. The bombers went in at altitudes between 12,000 and 20,000 feet, dropping 2,515 tons of incendiaries and destroying over three square miles of the northern sector of the town. Many Japanese fighters were in the air and, despite the strong Mustang escort, they pressed home determined attacks; ten B-29s were destroyed and sixty-four damaged. The B-29 gunners and the escorting fighters claimed eighteen enemy aircraft destroyed.

A pair of P-51Ds scrambling from Iwo.

The next three area incendiary attacks were carried out at night, but on 29 May XXI Bomber Command launched a final series of daylight incendiary raids, the first target being Yokohama. On this occasion the bombers were escorted by 101 Mustangs, and when about 150 enemy fighters – mostly Zeros – tried to break up the bomber formations the Mustangs shot down twenty-six of them for the loss of three of their own number.

The next attack, on 1 June against Osaka, was a disaster for VII Fighter Command. Severe thunderstorms were encountered by the 149 Mustangs that set out from Iwo Jima en route to the rendezvous point and twenty-seven were lost, many as the result of mid-air collisions. Only about thirty of the entire fighter force managed to struggle through to Osaka, their pilots utterly

exhausted and in no fit shape to give adequate protection to the bombers. Fortunately, Japanese fighter opposition was light. Because of this severe loss, 473 B-29s went to Kobe on 5 June without fighter escort and were subjected to 647 individual attacks by Japanese interceptors. Two B-29s were shot down and 176 damaged. The Mustangs were once again airborne in strength on 7 June, when 138 fighters carried out an escort mission to Osaka, but the American pilots found the city shrouded in dense cloud and no enemy fighters were airborne.

Meanwhile, operating from their bases in the Philippines, the Mustang groups of V Fighter Command had been heavily involved in the campaign to sever Japan's most important lifeline, joining other Fifth Air Force aircraft in attacks on enemy shipping in the South China Sea. This work normally involved escorting B-24 and B-25 bombers, but the Mustangs also undertook frequent fighter sweeps to Formosa and China. When Japanese fighters appeared they were destroyed, so that by the beginning of April 1945 Japanese air strength had been reduced to such an extent that few enemy ships had air cover. In the words of one Japanese convoy commander, Captain Tokuma Abe: 'When we requested air cover, only American aircraft showed up.' By this time, the attacks on Formosa had compelled the Japanese to withdraw most of their surviving aircraft to bases on the China coast; as the campaign continued they were forced to pull back even further, to Shanghai and Kyushu.

It had become obvious in March 1945 that it would be difficult to blockade the China Sea effectively without destroying the enemy air bases along the coast, which sheltered the last aircraft that could be used by the Japanese to protect their convoys, and also the strongly defended harbours which were being used as a refuge by enemy shipping. On 20 March permission was granted for aircraft of the Fifth, Thirteenth and Fourteenth Air Forces to begin attacking targets on the Chinese mainland once other commitments had

been met. The approved targets were Japanese installations and air bases in specific areas along the China and Indo-China coasts, the railroad between Saigon and Tourane, waterfront areas and supply bases at Hong Kong, Saigon and Canton, and other targets designated by General Chennault. Many of these raids were escorted by Mustangs of the 35th and 348th Fighter Groups, but contact with enemy fighters was now a rare occurrence. The last fighter encounter in this area for V Fighter Command came on 2 April, when Mustangs claimed one Oscar destroyed and two probables.

When the capture of Okinawa began to fall behind schedule after the landings in April, the seizure of the neighbouring island of Ie Shima, where there were three Japanese airstrips, was accelerated. Marines went ashore on 16 April and the objective was quickly secured. Aircraft needed to support the ground campaign on Okinawa had priority use of the captured airfield facilities; the fields on Okinawa itself were lightly surfaced and badly damaged, but the strip at Yontan was quickly patched up and US Marine fighters were soon able to operate from it. The situation was worse at Kadena, but the airstrip had been repaired to a sufficient standard to permit its use for all-weather operations at the beginning of May.

15th Fighter Group P-51Ds, taking off on a mission.

A pair of well-polished 21st FG P-51Ds taxying.

In mid-May, the strength of the Mustang force in the Pacific Operational Area was boosted by the arrival of the 506th Fighter Group, which arrived on Iwo Jima with the 457th, 458th and 462nd Fighter Squadrons, in time to join the other two Mustang groups in escorting XXI Bomber Command on the final series of daylight urban incendiary attacks. The last of these raids was carried out on 15 June, when the bombers returned to Osaka. On this occasion the skies were clear, and the city was razed from end to end.

XXI Bomber Command now turned its attention to a new series of daylight precision attacks on the Japanese aircraft industry, and in parallel with this the Mustang groups joined carrier-based aircraft in intensive strikes on enemy airfields, the aim still being to reduce the Kamikaze threat to negligible proportions. Although steps for the use of atomic bombs against key Japanese targets were now well advanced, it was still envisaged that a massive seaborne assault might have to be mounted against the Japanese home islands, and the havoc that could be wrought by the mere handful of suicide

aircraft that managed to break through the Allied fighter screen had been well demonstrated during the battle of Okinawa. The Kamikaze threat dictated the course of Allied air tactics in the Pacific at this stage in the same way that the Me 262 threat had influenced the latter stages of the air war in Europe, although the destructive potential of the suicide aircraft was far greater.

As an aside, it is interesting to note that rigid security regulations had created problems in basing the atomic bomb unit in the Pacific Operational Area. HQ Allied Air Forces POA first learned of the high priority accorded to the 509th Composite Bomb Group, the unit specially formed for the atomic task, in late January 1945, when steps were taken to secure base facilities for the group on Tinian. When a formal request was made to CINCPOA for the assignment of a priority for the required construction and shipping, approval was refused because the information furnished was unsatisfactory. A naval officer from Washington, however, eventually gave CINCPOA a somewhat delayed briefing on the mission of the 509th Group, and by

This photograph illustrates the problems of volcanic ash, a constant menace on Iwo Jima.

mid-June it was ready for operations from Tinian under the control of XXI Bomber Command.

By the beginning of July 1945 the number of Mustangs in the POA had risen to 348. AAFPOA's fighter assets now comprised two theatre groups, the 15th and 21st, and two Twentieth Air Force groups, the 414th (P-47N Thunderbolt) and 506th (P-51D Mustang) which flew B-29 escort missions from Iwo Jima under the operational control of XXI Bomber Command. At the

21st Fighter Group P-51s lined up on Iwo Jima.

Ground crews run up the engines prior to a day's flying. The Merlin's reliability was ably demonstrated on the long over-water escort missions.

same time the P-47N-equipped 301st Fighter Wing (413th, 507th and 318th Groups) was flying from Ie Shima in the Ryukus under the operational control of the Seventh Air Force. The P-47N was the most numerous fighter type in the theatre at this time, 451 aircraft having been assigned.

The Mustang groups continued their escort and ground-attack missions during July 1945, although much of XXI Bomber Command's effort was not devoted to a comprehensive night campaign against the smaller industrial cities of Japan, beginning on 17/18 June. Between 7 April and 1 June, the three Mustang groups had claimed the destruction of 666 Japanese aircraft, almost all on the ground; Japan's capacity to wage any form of air war, including suicide attacks, was rapidly being neutralized.

On 10 and 14 July naval aircraft relieved the Mustangs of their ground-attack duties for a short period, 1,000 US and British carrier-borne fighter-bombers attacking

targets in the Tokyo area and on Hokkaido on each of those two days. On 24 and 28 July aircraft of the US Third Fleet attacked Kure on the Inland Sea, where they destroyed the still-powerful remnants of the Imperial Japanese Navy, lying immobilized through lack of fuel.

In co-ordination with the carrier strikes of 24 July, 625 B-29s escorted by Mustangs made daylight precision attacks against targets in the Nagoya and Osaka areas. Again, aircraft and aero-engine production plants were the main objectives. The first day of August brought devastating fire raids against four small cities in north-central Honshu, and on 5 August 179 heavy and medium bombers of the US Fifth and Seventh Air Forces, accompanied by 146 Mustangs from Okinawa, made a devastating attack with HE and napalm on the port of Tarumizu, Kyushu.

For some weeks, while the strategic air offensive against the Japanese home islands continued, lone B-29s had been departing at intervals from Tinian, their destination some islands still held by the Japanese. The B-29s would release a single 10,000 lb bomb nicknamed the 'Pumpkin', which was detonated in the air over the target. On 21 July 1945 a crew of the 393rd Squadron, 509th Composite Bomb Group, dropped a 'Pumpkin' over the marshalling yards at Kobe and then swung their B-29 away in a violent evasive manoeuvre which was far removed from standard bombing procedure.

The purpose of these strange activities at last became clear when, on 6 August, the 509th CBG destroyed Hiroshima with the world's first operational uranium bomb. Three days later, a plutonium weapon levelled Nagasaki.

On 14 August, 449 B-29s took off from their bases in the Marianas and made rendezvous with a 186-strong Mustang fighter escort. The bombers attacked the naval arsenal at Hikari, the Osaka army arsenal, the Marifu railyards, south-west of Hiroshima, and the Nippon Oil Company plant at Atikia. In contrast to the previous day, when three groups of P-47N Thunderbolts had encountered substantial

numbers of enemy aircraft during an escort mission to Yawata, the remnants of the Japanese Army Air Force were absent from the sky. Even as the bombers and their escorts flew homewards, President Harry S. Truman was announcing the unconditional surrender of Japan to the world. The operational career of the P-51 Mustang in World War Two was over.

Lightweight Mustangs

It was the operational requirements of the Pacific War that gave impetus to the development of a lightweight version of the Mustang, an aircraft which, while possessing sufficient range for lengthy escort missions, would have the ability to outfight any likely opponent at any altitude. It was, in effect, what would nowadays be called an air superiority fighter. The design that emerged was the XP-51F, which flew from Mines Field on 14 February 1944. To save structural weight, North American dispensed with anything that was not considered absolutely necessary, including two of the .50 machine guns. The undercarriage was redesigned with smaller wheels so that the wing root chord extensions, needed to

The P-51K Mustang was specifically designed for operations in the Pacific.

The XP-51F was a lightweight version of the Mustang.

house the wheels when retracted, could be eliminated. An improved type of bubble canopy was fitted, with plastic components which were used in some parts of the airframe.

Three XP-51F prototypes were ordered for evaluation by the USAAF, all with V-1650-7 engines driving three-bladed propellers. Two more XP-51Fs were in fact ordered under a revised contract, but these were completed as XP-51Gs.

NAA and USAAF plots who flew the XP-51F were delighted with it. It had an enormous reserve of power, it would climb at 7,500 feet per minute. It would go up to 45,000 feet and it had a top speed of 466 mph at 30,000 feet. It was also a ton lighter than the basic P-51D, although as it was designed to British load factors, which were not as critical as those demanded by the USAAF, it was not as strong. This, as NAA test pilot Bob Chilton explained, was a major stumbling block in securing production contracts for the aircraft.

'We were dealing with such a huge volume of new aircraft that time for testing new projects, unless they were of the highest priority, was strictly limited.

On an overall total, the XP-51Fs probably accumulated no more than 100 flying hours.

'The USAAF did not like the idea that the XP-51F was built to British loading specifications. They had gotten used to the incredibly rugged strength designed into almost all American fighters. They felt that the Japanese had gone way too far in sacrificing structural strength for additional performance. The USAAF was also none too pleased with the European and British practice of dropping some structural strength in favour of boosted performance. '

North American tried very hard to push the XP-51F's top speed past the 500 mph mark, but never succeeded in doing so. In the end the USAAF lost interest, and the XP-51F programme slipped into obscurity, although the third aircraft was shipped to England for testing at the A&AEE, Boscombe Down, with the RAF serial FR409.

The two aircraft ordered under the revised contract were completed as XP-51Gs, fitted with Rolls-Royce Merlin 145 engines driving five-bladed Rotol propellers. One of these aircraft was test flown by North American and the other, serialled FR410, was evaluated by the A&AEE. The XP-51G reached a maximum speed of 472 mph at 20,750 feet. The last lightweight Mustang experimental aircraft was the XP-51J, which was similar to the F and G except that it was fitted with the Allison V-1710-119 engine. Two aircraft were built and subjected to a brief test programme, the purpose being to evaluate this version of the Allison as a replacement for the Merlin in case Britain withdrew manufacturing rights from Packard after the war.

The ultimate Mustang was the P-51H, which incorporated many features of the lightweight models and which first flew on 3 February 1945. Fitted with a water-injected V-1650-9 engine developing 2,218 horsepower, it had a maximum speed of 487 mph at 25,000 feet, making it the fastest of all the Mustangs. The P-51H was intended primarily for service in the Pacific Operational Area and had the same armament, including external ordnance loads, as the P-51D. The USAAF ordered 1,445 examples from the Inglewood factory, but only 555 had been delivered at the time of Japan's surrender and the remainder of the contract was cancelled. Most of the aircraft already delivered served post-war with Air National Guard units.

The ultimate Mustang variant was the P-51H. It was assigned to a number of Air National Guard Units after World War Two.

Chapter 10
Mustangs in Post-War Service

T HE MUSTANG'S primary role of long-range escort fighter, which it had undertaken with such outstanding success during the war, was to remain in force for some time after the cessation of hostilities. On 21 March 1946, Strategic Air Command was formed within the framework of the United States Army Air Forces, 'to conduct long-range offensive operations in any part of the world either independently or in co-operation with land and Naval forces'. Among the resources assigned to the new Command was the 33rd Fighter Group, which had served in India during the war and which was now at Roswell Army Airfield, New Mexico, with a unit establishment of seventy-five P-51 Mustangs in three squadrons, the 58th, 59th and 60th Fighter Squadrons.

A second fighter group was assigned to SAC on 20 August 1946. This was the 27th FG, which was activated at Andrews Army Airfield on that date, but remained without aircraft for nearly a year. It received the first of its seventy-five Mustangs in July 1947, following a move to Kearney Army Airfield in Nebraska, a move that coincided with the formation of the United States Air Force as an independent Service. The 27th FG's three squadrons were the 522nd, 523rd and 524th FS. The third and last Mustang-equipped group to be assigned to SAC was the 82nd FG (95th, 96th and 97th FS) at Grenier Air Force Base (as the former Army Airfields were now designated) in New Hampshire. SAC also had two P-80 Shooting Star fighter groups assigned to it at this time, so that by the end of 1947 its fighter assets comprised, on paper at least, 230 P-51s and 120 P-80s.

The year 1948 saw a major restructuring of the USAF's fighter resources as the F-86 Sabre came on to the inventory. In December, the 33rd Fighter Group was removed from SAC control and re-assigned to Air Defense Command; it retained its Mustangs – now designated F-51s – until 1950, when it re-equipped with F-84 Thunderjets. Of the other Mustang units, the 27th FG transferred to Air Defense Command control in August 1949 and later re-equipped with F-84s. It was during this period that the USAF fighter groups were re-designated Tactical Fighter Wings.

Apart from the units mentioned above, many other USAAF/USAF groups/wings continued to use the Mustang for some time after the war. These were:

1st Tactical Fighter Wing. Although equipped with F-80 Shooting Stars, this unit operated some F-51s in 1951-2 when it was based at Norton AFB and responsible for the defence of southern California.
8th Tactical Reconnaissance Wing. Operated F-51s at Ashiya and Itazuke, Japan, before converting to F-80s in 1950.
10th Tactical Reconnaissance Wing. Operated F-51s and F-6s in 1947-8, then re-equipped with RF-51s until 1949 when it converted to RF-80s. Based at Pope AFB, North Carolina.
18th Tactical Fighter Wing. Operated F-51s from 1948 to 1953 at Clark AFB in the Philippines, Korea and Okinawa. Later converted to F-86s at Presque Isle, Maine.
20th Tactical Fighter Wing. Returned to the United States from England in October 1945 and was deactivated in November; it was reactivated at Shaw AFB, South

The Mustang saw widespread service with the Air National Guard post-war. Photographs show three ANG units which used the aircraft.

Carolina, and used F-51s in 1947-8 until re-equipment with F-84s.

23rd Tactical Fighter Wing. This unit remained in China until December 1945, then returned to the US to be deactivated in February 1946. It was reactivated and operated F-51s in the air defence of the north-eastern USA in 1951–2 before conversion to F-86s.

31st Tactical Fighter Wing. Deactivated on 7 November 1945 after its return to the US from Europe, this unit was reactivated in 1947 and operated F-51s until 1949, when it re-equipped with F-84s. Located at Turner AFB, Georgia.

35th Tactical Fighter Wing. This unit moved to Japan in October 1945 as part of the Allied Forces of Occupation at Johnson and Yokota AFBs. Converted to F-80s in 1950, but reverted to F-51s for Korean War operations. Re-equipped with F-86 Sabres in 1953.

49th Tactical Fighter Wing. A former P-38 Lightning unit which had operated throughout the Pacific campaigns, the 49th TFW used F-51s at Misawa, Japan, in 1948-50 before converting to F-80s.

50th Tactical Fighter Wing. This unit, based at Otis AFB, Massachusetts, used F-51s in 1948-50 before conversion to F-84s.

56th Tactical Fighter Wing. Based at Selfridge AFB, Michigan, this F-86 Sabre unit used a few F-51s in 1951-2.

78th Tactical Fighter Wing. Based at Hamilton AFB, California, this unit was responsible for the air defence of the US Pacific coast and was equipped with F-51s from 1949 to 1952.

81st Tactical Fighter Wing. This unit, based at Larson AFB, Washington, was equipped with F-86s but still had a few F-51s on its inventory in 1951.

340th Tactical Fighter Wing. This unit, assigned to the Eleventh Air Force in Alaska, exchanged its P-38s for P-51s in 1946 and used the Mustangs for a few months before being deactivated in August of that year.

347th Tactical Fighter Wing. One of the units forming the Allied Occupation Forces in Japan, the 347th operated F-51s, F-61s and F-82s in 1949-50. It was based at Itazuke, Ashiya and Nagoya.

366th Tactical Fighter Wing. This unit used some F-51s while working up on F-86 Sabres at England AFB, Louisiana, in 1953.

368th Tactical Fighter Group. This wartime P-47 unit was redesignated the 136th Fighter Group after the war and assigned to the Texas Air National Guard. It was called to active service in October 1950 and assigned to Tactical Air Command. Re-designated the 136th Fighter-Bomber Wing, it used F-51s until early 1951, when it converted to F-84s.

370th Fighter Group. This unit returned to the US from Europe in October 1945, was re-designated the 140th Fighter Group and assigned to the Colorado Air National Guard in 1946. Equipped with F-51s, it was called to active duty on 1 April 1951 and was re-designated the 140th Fighter-Bomber Wing in May that year, re-equipping with F-84s.

373rd Fighter Group. Another wartime P-47 unit, the 373rd FG was re-designated the 146th Fighter Group post-war, equipped with F-51s and assigned to the California Air National Guard. It was called to active service on 1 April 1951 and assigned to Strategic Air Command for the duration of the Korean War.

445th Fighter-Bomber Wing (Composite). Based at Buffalo, NY, this reserve unit used F-51s to maintain operational proficiency as a fighter-bomber unit from 1952 to 1956. It later transferred to the Military Air Transport Service.

452nd Tactical Reconnaissance Wing. Based at Long Beach AFB, California, the 452nd TRW used F-51s and TF-51s in the reserve TacR role, 1953-4.

475th Fighter Wing. Based at Itazuke and Ashiya, Japan, as part of the Allied

Chinese Nationalist P-51Ds. For some reason the national insignia has been obliterated.

Occupation Forces, this unit used F-51s in 1948-9 until its deactivation.

479th Fighter-Bomber Wing. Based at George AFB, California, the 479th FBW used F-51s in 1952-3 while working up on F-86 Sabres.

The above list represents the principal USAF units to use the Mustang in the post-war years; many others operated small numbers of F-51s to maintain combat proficiency, for fast communications and so on.

The Mustang saw little wartime service outside the USAAF and RAF, but it was widely used by other nations during the post-war years. Even before the war ended, fifty P-51Ds were supplied to China and forty to Holland for use by the Netherlands East India Air Force. The F-51D Mustangs were used by the Kuomintang (Chinese Nationalist) forces in the 1946-49 civil war against the Communists, but no record exists of their operations. Additional Mustangs were supplied to the Kuomintang during this period; many of them fell into the hands of the victorious Communists or were surrendered by defecting Nationalist pilots, and some were used by the Chinese People's Liberation Air Force as advanced trainers until well into the 1950s.

The Dutch P-51D Mustangs equipped two squadrons of the Netherlands East India Air Force and operated alongside P-40s and, on the orders of the colonial authorities, operated against the forces of the Republic of Indonesia, which had been proclaimed on 17 August 1945 at the time of the Japanese surrender. Combat aircraft, albeit in a very poor state of maintenance, were among the Japanese equipment seized by the Indonesians, and although these were very rarely used operationally against the Dutch, a Mitsubishi Ki 51 light bomber attacked Semarang on 29 July 1947, leading to a series of airfield attacks by the Mustangs and Kittyhawks in which the remaining Japanese aircraft were destroyed.

Royal New Zealand Air Force P-51Ds.

With the cessation of hostilities and the transfer of sovereignty to the Indonesian Republic in 1949, the Indonesian Air Force (AURI) began to expand with Dutch aid. The bulk of the equipment of the two F-51D fighter-bomber squadrons was transferred to it and, together with some B-25 Mitchells and PBY-5A Catalinas, these aircraft formed No 1 Squadron, which became the AURI's operational element. It was not long before the new organization had its first test; in 1950 a rebellion broke out on the remote island of Ambon, the object being to form a separate Republic of the South Moluccas. The Mustangs and Mitchells strafed and destroyed the rebel defences with bombs, rockets and machine guns, successfully paving the way for a landing by Indonesian ground forces.

AURI F-51D and K Mustangs took part in several internal police actions during the years that followed. Some were still in use in the early 1960s, during the period of confrontation with Malaysia; in 1963 they penetrated Malaysian air space in North Borneo on several occasions, escorting B-25 bombers engaged in leaflet-dropping missions. These incursions ceased when a squadron of RAF Hunter jet fighters was deployed to Borneo.

While the Second World War was still in progress, the Royal Australian Air Force had selected the P-51D Mustang for licence production to meet an urgent need for a new long-range fighter to equip its squadrons operating in the south-west Pacific. One complete airframe was acquired, together with 100 sets of assemblies; eighty of these were assembled by the Commonwealth Aircraft Corporation as CA-17 Mustang Mk XXs. All aircraft in this initial batch were powered by the V-1650-3 Packard-Merlin engine, the first flying on 29 April 1945. Licence production aircraft comprised forty CA-18 Mustang Mk XXIs with V-1650-7 engines, fourteen Mustang XXIIs with F24 oblique cameras mounted in the fuselage and sixty-six Mustang XXIIIs with British-built Rolls-Royce Merlin 66 or 70 engines. Production of another 300 Mustangs in Australia was cancelled, and instead the RAAF acquired 214 P-51Ds and eighty-four P-51Ks from USAAF stocks. None of these aircraft had reached operational status by the time the Pacific war ended.

It is worth noting that at this time, the Commonwealth Aircraft Corporation was testing an indigenous design, the CA-15 fighter, which resembled the Mustang in

Royal Swedish Air Force P-51D (J-26).

many design features and which was also intended for service in the Pacific Theatre. It was too late to see operational service and only one prototype was completed, flying for the first time on 4 March 1946 powered by a Rolls-Royce Griffon 61 engine. It reached a speed of 448 mph at 26,400 feet and underwent a limited test programme until 1950, when it was broken up.

On 19 December 1945, the Australian War Cabinet decided that Australia should contribute Army, Navy and RAAF units to the British Commonwealth Occupation Forces in Japan under the overall command of General Douglas MacArthur. The air component of the Occupation Force was organised into a tactical group known as the British Commonwealth Air Force (BCAIR) and included one single-engined fighter wing made up of two RAF Spitfire squadrons and an RNZAF Corsair squadron, one single-engined fighter wing comprising three RAAF Mustang squadrons, and one squadron of the RAF Regiment.

The RAAF assigned No 81 Wing, whose Nos 76, 77 and 82 Squadrons were then based a Labuan, North Borneo, and in the process of converting to Mustangs. The Wing's base in Japan was to be Iwakuni, 450 miles west of Tokyo on the Inland Sea. The main body of No 81 Wing left Labuan by sea on 11 February 1946, followed later in the month by the Mustangs. No 76 Squadron was the first to move, leaving on the 28th and arriving at Bofu on 9 March. On 2 March No 82 Squadron also left Labuan for Japan, unfortunately losing three Mustangs, together with an escorting Mosquito, in extremely bad weather somewhere off Cape Tsuru, Kyushu. By 21 March No 77 Squadron had also arrived at Bofu. The entire Wing remained there until reconstruction work at Iwakuni was completed, then moved up to its new base.

The primary task of No 81 Wing at Iwakuni was to fly surveillance patrols over Yamaguchi, Hiroshima, Tottori and Shimane Prefectures and Shikoku Island. In 1949 Nos 76 and 82 Squadrons were withdrawn to Australia, leaving No 77 Squadron to maintain the RAAF's presence in Japan. It was still there in the summer of 1950, when, as we shall see later, it was to play a vital and gallant role in support of United Nations forces in the Korean War.

One of the biggest post-war overseas Mustang customers was the Royal Swedish Air Force. Several Mustangs had made emergency landings in Sweden during the war, and in April 1945 two of these aircraft (43-6365 of the 357th FG and 43-6461 of the 339th FG) were taken on RSAF charge and designated J26. Both were P-51Bs. Swedish pilots who flew the Mustang were highly impressed by its performance, and contracts were placed for the delivery of 157 P-51Ds. Deliveries were completed by March 1948, the Mustangs serving with F4 Wing at Östersund and F16 Wing at Uppsala. In 1951 twelve of the J26s were converted for photo-reconnaissance and designated S26; these aircraft served with F21 Wing at Lulea.

In 1952, with the RSAF's fighter wings re-equipping with jet aircraft, the Mustangs were put up for sale. Most went to Latin American countries (see below), but in September 1952 Israel signed a contract with Sweden for the delivery of twenty-five Mustangs for service with the Israeli Defence Forces/Air Force. The Mustangs were handed over between November 1952 and June 1953 and went into service with the IDF/AF's No 102 Squadron, a unit specialising in ground attack work. (Nos 101 and 103 Squadrons were respectively fighter and transport units.) The IDF/AF Mustangs were in action almost continuously during Israel's lightning campaign against Egyptian forces in the Sinai Desert, which began on 29 October 1956. In fact they flew the first mission of the campaign. At 1500 hours on D-Day, a couple of hours before an Israeli paratroop battalion was due to be dropped on the strategic Mitla Pass, two Mustang pilots were given the task of cutting the Egyptian telephone wires running from Kuseima to

Mustangs, mostly ex-Swedish aircraft, played a key role in the Israeli Air Force's victory in Sinai in 1956.

Nahel and from El Thamad to Mitla. The aircraft were fitted with special hooks, trailing at the end of a cable deployed from a small winch under their wings. This apparatus was designed to catch the telephone wires and tear them apart. It failed to work so the Mustang pilots sliced through the wires with the leading edges of their wings and returned to base with no worse damage than a few dents.

In the afternoon of 30 October the Israeli Air Force launched heavy attacks on Egyptian reinforcements attempting to advance into Sinai from the Canal Zone. Twenty Mustangs attacked enemy columns on the east bank of the Canal with bombs and rockets and also provided support for the Israeli Central Task Force's assault on Kuseima, where some of the heaviest fighting of the initial phase of the campaign was taking place. Two Mustangs were shot down by intense ground fire.

The main problem facing the Israeli ground attack pilots during this early phase was an almost complete lack of communication between the ground units and the air force. Vital signalling equipment had been destroyed during the battle for Kuseima, with the result that the Central Task Force had been unable to request air support when it needed it most. Worse still, Israeli units had been attacked three times by their own aircraft, which had knocked out one half-track and damaged several other vehicles. Fortunately, there had been no serious casualties. By the morning of D plus 2, however, air-ground liaison had once again been established, and the Egyptian units were subjected to a well-directed onslaught by Ouragans, Mustangs and Harvards. Two Mustangs and one Harvard were damaged, but they all returned safely to base.

Later in the day, an Egyptian armoured column at Bir Gifgafa was attacked by a flight of three Mustangs, led by Captain Paz. They dropped their napalm and returned to make several strafing runs; their 0.5 machine guns were ineffective against the armour of the enemy tanks, but they caused considerable damage to a group of soft-skinned vehicles. The attacks were made through heavy fire and Captain Paz's Mustang was hit. Black smoke filled the cockpit and the oil pressure dropped rapidly. He climbed to 1,000 feet and headed away from the enemy concentration, electing to make a belly landing.

Paz picked a patch of ground that was relatively free from large boulders and set the Mustang down on it, emerging from the forced landing with nothing worse than a severe shaking. He crawled along a nearby Wadi and hid among some bushes, where he lay low till nightfall. There was no sign of any Egyptians, but he decided not to take any risks. As soon as darkness fell, he set off to walk in the direction of Bir Hasana, where he hoped to join up with Israeli forces. He reached it before first light, only to find the place still occupied by the Egyptians. There was no alternative but to continue walking, north-eastwards this time, towards Jebel Libni. He eventually reached his goal after marching for thirty hours through the desert, collapsing exhausted into the arms of an Israeli patrol. During his marathon trek, his rations had consisted of less than a pint of water and a few sweets, together with a few desert leaves which he had chewed for their juices.

In the course of the day the Mustang pilots made sortie after sortie against the enemy column at Bir Gifgafa, on the central road to Sinai, and inflicted considerable damage on the Egyptian 1st Armoured Brigade. This was known as the 'Soviet Brigade' because it was equipped exclusively with Russian tanks and self-propelled guns; it was also strongly defended by mobile anti-aircraft artillery, so that every attack had to be pressed home through heavy fire.

The Mustangs, because of their lower attack speed and the position of their ventral radiator, were particularly vulnerable, and most returned to base with varying degrees of battle damage. The

Mustangs, however, made their runs at very low altitude, and the Egyptian anti-aircraft gunners appeared to have difficulty in depressing their weapons to a sufficient degree. On at least two occasions, while firing shells across the desert at an attacking aircraft, they hit their own vehicles that came into the line of fire. During strikes flown later in the day, the Mustang pilots went after the guns and put several out of action.

The Israeli pilots took incredible risks to make sure of destroying their objectives, and a strafing run nearly ended in disaster for one Mustang pilot when he dived on an ammunition truck, firing as he closed in to point-blank range. The truck exploded and he was caught in the blast; his aircraft was hurled bodily upwards and missed colliding with a second aircraft by a matter of inches. Of the six Mustangs that took part in this attack, five were damaged by ground fire or flying debris, but all were patched up within an hour of their return to base. By the end of the day the forward elements of the lst Armoured Brigade had reached Bir Rod Salim, twenty miles west of Jebel Libni, but the main body was still in the Gifgafa area. The road was littered with the wreckage of ninety tanks, trucks and personnel carriers, almost all the victims of the Mustangs.

In the early hours of 1 November, Israeli forces launched an assault on Rafah at the southern end of the Gaza Strip. Mustangs and Ouragans attacked the enemy positions with rockets and napalm at first light, and at 0800 hours the Egyptian commander ordered his hard-pressed units to withdraw to El Arish, leaving Rafah in Israeli hands. Some time later the airfield at El Arish was strafed by Mustangs and Ouragans, which attacked three MiG-15s and one Mraz Sokol light aircraft on the ground. The MiGs were later found to be dummies, but the Sokol was real enough and was destroyed.

By the morning of 2 November, it was obvious that the Egyptian forces in Sinai were in full retreat. The 1st Armoured Brigade began to move back from Bir

Gifgafa at dawn, covering the tail-end of the withdrawal, and was subjected to continual air attacks by Mustangs and Ouragans all the way back to the Suez Canal. In all, the aircraft destroyed twenty-two T-34 tanks, five SU-100 self-propelled guns and at least thirty-five armoured personnel carriers.

Meanwhile, an Israeli Eastern Task Force had begun a long advance southwards along the Gulf of Aqaba towards Sharm el Sheikh. This objective, together with nearby Ras Nasarini, commanded the Straits of Tiran; both positions were strongly fortified and possessed heavy anti-aircraft defences. From first light on 2 November both these positions were subjected to heavy air strikes by Mustangs, Ouragans and Mysteres, and at noon on the following day five Mustangs showered the Egyptian defences at Ras Nasarini with napalm in what was meant to be a softening-up attack prior to an assault by the Israeli 9th Infantry Brigade. On their return to base, the pilots reported that there had been a complete lack of anti-aircraft fire. It was hardly surprising; the 400-strong garrison had already fallen back on Sharm el Sheikh, having spiked their guns. The Israeli column pressed on and arrived opposite the perimeter of Sharm el Sheikh at 1400 hours. The leading elements were pinned down by heavy fire from an outpost, but it gave no more trouble after two Mustangs hit it with thirty-two rockets an hour later.

The IAF made several more attacks on Sharm el Sheikh during the remainder of the afternoon while the Israeli ground forces regrouped and refuelled in readiness for the final assault. The air strikes had done their work well, in spite of intense and highly accurate anti-aircraft fire, and caused many casualties, most of whom were evacuated by sea in small craft after nightfall. Nevertheless, the first Israeli attack, which opened at 0330 hours on 5 November, was quickly pinned down by heavy Egyptian fire. The Israelis withdrew after sustaining some losses and attacked again at 0700 hours with Mustangs, Ouragans and Mysteres strafing ahead of them in an almost continuous 'cab-rank'. After a two-hour battle that saw some of the most savage hand-to-hand fighting of the entire campaign, the Egyptian garrison finally surrendered at 0900 hours.

At 1130 hours the Israeli Air Force mounted its last strike of the campaign when Mustangs and Ouragans attacked the small island of Sanafir, adjacent to Tiran about two miles offshore, and pounded it with rockets and napalm for about twenty minutes. When Israeli troops landed, they found the island deserted.

Israeli Mustang losses in the Sinai campaign amounted to nine aircraft, three times as many as any other Israeli type and about thirty per cent of the effective Mustang force. As part of the overall assessment of the part played by the Israeli Air Force in the campaign, it was decided to replace the piston-engined aircraft still in first-line service with modern jet types as quickly as possible; to this end an order was placed with the French government for the purchase of an additional forty-five Dassault Ouragans; these began to arrive in February 1957, permitting the retirement of the ageing Mustangs. Three of the latter are today preserved at the Israeli Air Force Museum, Hazerim, as a tribute to the part played by the type in assuring Israel's survival. Another Israeli Mustang (26020, ex-USAAF 44-63992) was returned to Sweden in 1966, restored in the colours

P-51D Mustangs in service with the Royal Canadian Air Force.

P-51D in Swiss Air Force markings.

of F16 Wing and placed on display at the Swedish Air Force Museum, Malmen. Yet another, serial unknown, is stored at Tees-side Airport near Darlington, County Durham, in pieces and awaiting restoration.

The Mustang's good all-round perform-ance as an interceptor and a ground-attack

The Philippines used the Mustang as first-line equipment until 1960.

During the war, the Mustang's suitability for carrier operations was assessed. The 'one-off' aircraft (serial 44-14017) is seen here during deck landing trials on the USS *Shangri-La*. The pilot was Lt R.M. Elder, USN.

aircraft, together with the fact that it was available in large quantities at cut prices, made it an attractive purchase for countries whose air arms were seeking to equip with jet aircraft in the immediate post-war years. Among them was the Royal Canadian Air Force (as it then was) which was looking to re-equip its fighter squadrons with the F-86 Sabre. Canada purchased 100 ex-USAAF F-15D Mustangs in 1945 and these remained first-line equipment until the early 1950s, when deliveries of Canadair-built Sabres began. Even then, the Mustang remained on the inventory as the equipment of six RCAF auxiliary squadrons, and was not retired until 1956.

Switzerland also acquired 100 surplus Mustangs in 1948 while awaiting the delivery of de Havilland Vampire FB.Mk.6 jet fighters. The Mustangs, all P-51Ds, permitted the withdrawal of the *Flugwaffe*'s last surviving Messerschmitt Bf 109Es in 1949, and remained in first-line service until 1956 when re-equipment with Vampires was complete.

The Italian Air Force used forty-eight F-51D Mustangs between 1948 and 1953, thirty were delivered to the Royal New Zealand Air Force in 1945-6, and the type equipped No 2 'Cheetah' Squadron of the South African Air Force, which fought with distinction in the Korean War. The Philippines, too, received P-51Ds in 1946 and used them until 1960.

Latin America provided a ready market for surplus Mustangs post-war, albeit in relatively small numbers. Cuba received some F-51Ds in 1947 and these continued in service until they were replaced with Soviet equipment in 1960. Some were used in action by the Batista government against Fidel Castro's revolutionary forces in 1959, but there is no record of these operations. Nicaragua equipped one fighter squadron with twenty-six ex-Swedish F-51Ds in 1954, operating alongside a fighter-bomber squadron equipped with F-47D Thunderbolts, and both units used these types until 1964. Uruguay also had a squadron of F-51Ds until 1960, when the

The Cavalier Mustang II, a turboprop-powered conversion for counter-insurgency operations.

Mustangs were replaced by F-80C Shooting Stars; Mustangs equipped a fighter-bomber squadron of the Guatemalan Air Force until the mid-1960s; F-51Ds formed part of a composite squadron of the Haitian Air Corps at Bowen Field, Port-au-Prince, and were used for internal policing until 1975, when the last six examples were retired; and Honduras used a small number of F-51Ds until 1959, when they were replaced by ten refurbished F4U-5 Corsairs pending the arrival of jet equipment.

But for length of service with the Mustang the honour must go to the Dominican Aviation Corps, which purchased forty-two F-51Ds from Sweden, along with a number of Vampire F.1s, in 1952. The last twelve aircraft, completely refurbished, were still operating from Santo Domingo until 1984, when they were retired and sold off to private owners. They were the last operational examples of the 14,819 Mustangs built since the prototype first flew in 1941, forty-three years earlier. There could be no finer tribute to a remarkable aircraft.

The Cavalier Mustang

Some of the F-51D Mustangs supplied to Latin American countries after 1967, as replacements for surplus USAF aircraft, were built by the Cavalier Aircraft Corporation and supplied to client states by the US government under a project known as Peace Condor for use as counter-insurgency aircraft. The aircraft were assembled from component parts, some manufactured as new and others taken from stocks. The Company held large stocks of Mustang components and also spares for the Rolls-Royce Merlin engine,

being the western hemisphere distributor for the latter.

The Cavalier Mustangs used the existing F-51D wings and fuselage but the tail fin was fourteen inches taller, being similar to that introduced on the P-51H in 1945. Like the P-51D, the aircraft carried an armament of six 0.50 machine guns in the wings; the main spars were reinforced and there were four hardpoints under each wing. The inboard hardpoints could each carry one 1,000 lb bomb or 110-gallon fuel tank; the other six positions carried 5-inch HVARs which could be fired in salvo or individually. British Mk IIIN gun sights were installed, produced for the Hawker Hunter and purchased as surplus. Avionics were based on the Bendix lightweight solid state series, and included the T-12C ADF radio compass, RN-222A VHF/VOR receiver and dual RT-221A-28 VHF transceivers. The engine was a 1,490 horsepower Packard V-1650-7, the equivalent of the Merlin 69.

Cavalier also produced a two-seat trainer version, the TF-51D, which was basically similar to the TP-51D of 1944. The trainer was equipped to the same standard as the fighter-bomber, but wing armament was reduced to four guns.

Cavalier also developed two further variants of the basic F-51D, the Mustang II – which had a heavier ordnance load, wingtip tanks and a 1,760 horsepower Merlin 620 engine – and the Turbo Mustang III, which was fitted with a Rolls-Royce Dart 510 engine. Both were intended to replace earlier P-51s in the counter-insurgency role, but in most Latin American air arms this requirement was met by jet equipment such as the Cessna A-37, which had proved itself in Vietnam.

Chapter 11
The F-82 Twin Mustang

BY THE SUMMER of 1943, Japanese expansion in the Pacific had been checked. Enemy forces were literally at the gates of Australia and India, but they were to go no further. Both sides sought to strengthen their forces and positions in readiness for the battles that lay ahead, turning 1943 into a year of consolidation, but in this aim the Japanese were at a disadvantage. First, their shipyards could not match the output of American yards, which in 1943 alone put into service a warship tonnage equivalent to that of the

total Imperial Japanese Navy at the outset of the Pacific War; second, while American industry could replace the air losses suffered during the bitter fighting for the island of Guadalcanal, the Japanese could not; and third, because of that battle, the Japanese had lost the strategic initiative.

The principal weakness of Japanese strategic policy was that, without the means to defeat the Americans in the air and at sea, any Japanese island garrison could be subjected to overwhelming attack and reduced over a period of time, or

The F-82 Twin Mustang.

The F-82 Twin Mustang.

simply bypassed by an enemy who could choose his course of operations depending on the prevailing circumstances.

The Americans decided to do both. Supported by powerful task forces, land forces would drive across the Pacific, capturing those islands which had a strategic value and bypassing others of less worth whose capture would have involved many needless casualties. Dictating the whole of this strategic policy was the requirement to seize islands as close as possible to Japan, islands that could be turned into bases from which the full might of strategic air warfare could be unleashed on the Japanese war economy.

The bomber that was to carry out the strategic air offensive, the Boeing B-29, was already in priority production. It was a far different aircraft from the B-17 that was engaged in the strategic air offensive against Germany; nevertheless, its heavy

defensive armament alone could not be relied upon to ward off determined fighter attacks during daylight bombing operations, so there was a clear requirement for a long-range fighter escort. The P-51 Mustang had the required combat radius to accompany the B-29s when, in due course, they would be operating from locations in the Marianas island group, but the problem with the P-51 was that it was a single-seater and not therefore well suited to long-range missions requiring precise navigation over water. Pilot fatigue was another consideration on such missions.

In the late summer of 1943, North American Aviation Inc began design work on a fighter that would meet this requirement. The concept was simple enough, involving the joining of two P-51H fuselages by means of a new wing centre section and creating a two-seat, twin-engined aircraft with considerably enhanced long-range performance.

The new configuration, by making provision for two pilots, would greatly ease the strain of lengthy over-water flights, and the two engines would increase the safety margin. North American gave the project the designation NA-120 and submitted the scheme to the USAAF, who liked it and issued contract AC-2029, covering the manufacture of two prototypes, on 7 January 1944. Now designated XP-82, the new aircraft was to be powered by two Packard-built Rolls-Royce Merlin V-1650-23/25 engines with their propellors rotating in opposite directions, so virtually eliminating any torque.

Although the twin fuselages were basically those of a P-51H, they underwent so many modifications that they emerged as virtually a new design. Each fuselage was fitted with an individual tail wheel, the main undercarriage legs being attached to the root of the outer wing panels and retracting into the wing centre section, which also housed the armament of six 0.50 calibre machine guns. There was also provision for the carriage of fuel tanks, bombs or rockets on the outer wing panels. In addition, a large pod containing eight 0.50 calibre guns and their ammunition could be attached under the wing centre section, giving the aircraft a formidable forward firing armament, if need be, of fourteen heavy-calibre machine guns.

Three prototypes were planned, two of them XP-82s with Packard Merlin engines and the other, designated XP-82A, with Allison V-1710-119 engines equipped with propellers that rotated in the same direction. This third aircraft was to be built as an insurance against the British government cancelling Packard's licence to build the Merlin once hostilities were over. The production variant was to be designated P-82B, and 500 were ordered in a USAAF contract issued on 8 March 1944.

The necessary jigs and tools were quickly set up at North American's Inglewood plant, and the first aircraft were nearing completion on the assembly line when America's use of the atomic bomb brought the war in the Pacific to an abrupt end. One immediate consequence was that the order for 500 Twin Mustangs was cut back to just twenty examples for service with the USAF Air Defense Command. Eighteen were completed as P-82Bs, but the tenth and eleventh production aircraft were completed as P-82C and P-82D night fighters for evaluation as replacements for the Northrop P-61 Black Widow in this role. The P-82C (44-65169) was fitted with an SCR720 AI radar in a large central pod, while the P-82D (44-65170) carried the APS-4. The radar operator sat in the right-hand cockpit at his AI console, the radar aerials being installed under the outer wing sections.

Of the eighteen P-82Bs, one was destined to enter the annals of aviation history. This was 44-65168 'Betty Jo', named after the wife of the pilot Lt Col Robert E.Thacker. On 27 February 1947, with co-pilot Lt John Ard, Thacker made a record-breaking flight from Hickam Field, Hawaii, to New York in fourteen hours thirty-three minutes, covering a distance of 5,051 miles at an average speed of 334 mph. It was a noteworthy achievement, expecially since three of the aircraft's four fuel tanks would not jettison, causing extra drag and making the P-82 unstable. The flight was also indicative of what the Twin Mustang might have accomplished had it been called upon to fill its role of long-range escort fighter under combat conditions. Colonel Thacker was a very experienced pilot, having served in both theatres during the war; on 7 December 1941 he had taken part in the flight of thirteen B-17 Flying Fortresses which, having left Hamilton Field in California, landed at Hickam during the height of the Japanese attack on Pearl Harbor.

Meanwhile, trials with the P-82C and P-82D had shown that these night-fighter, all-weather variants of the Twin Mustang would make good replacements for the P-61, and in March 1946 orders were placed for an additional 250 aircraft. However, the first 100 of these (46-255 to 46-354) were to be completed as escort and ground-attack fighters for service with the newly-established Strategic Air Command. When the Command came into existence on 21 March 1946 its material assets were slender. For escort duties there were two fighter groups, the 4th and 56th; the first had seventy-five P-51 Mustangs but the other, as yet, had no aircraft at all.

By the end of 1947 SAC's fighter resources had expanded to five groups, each with an establishment of seventy-five aircraft, three equipped with P-51s and two with P-80 Shooting Stars, but in 1948 this was again reduced to two groups, one with F-51s (the 'P' prefix now having given way to 'F' in the USAF designation system) and the other with F-82Es, as the new escort version of the Twin Mustang was designated. The F-82E continued to serve with the 27th Fighter Escort Group until early in 1950, when it began to be replaced by the Republic F-84E Thunderjet. Like all other Twin Mustangs produced post-war the F-82E was powered by Allison engines.

Of the remaining Twin Mustangs, ninety-one were completed as F-82F night-fighters with APS-4 radar and fifty-nine as F-82Gs with SCR-720 radar. These aircraft, which were also fitted with APN-1 radar altimeters and APS-13 tail warning radars, equipped the 51st Fighter Interceptor Group (16th, 25th and 26th Squadrons), the 52nd All-Weather Fighter Group (2nd and 5th Squadrons), the 325th All-Weather Fighter Group (317th, 318th and 319th Squadrons) and the 84th Reserve Fighter Group (496th, 497th and 498th Squadrons).

In the Far East, Twin Mustangs were also assigned to the 4th Fighter Squadron (All-Weather) at Naha on Okinawa, the 68th Fighter Squadron (All-Weather) at Itazuke on Kyushu, and the 339th Fighter Squadron (All-Weather) at Yokota, near Tokyo. In 1953, the surviving Twin Mustangs belonging to these units would be withdrawn and sent to Alaska to form USAF's last F-82 unit, the 449th Fighter Interceptor Squadron, where they were to serve in the Arctic air defence role until their replacement with the Northrop F-89 Scorpion.

But before that, the Twin Mustang and its single-engined forebear were to write an indelible and valiant chapter in the story of the air war over Korea.

Chapter 12
The Mustang in the Korean War

WHEN NORTH KOREA attacked across the 38th parallel at dawn on 25 June 1950, one fact that became quickly apparent was the woefully inadequate state of the Republic of Korea Air Force (ROKAF) to meet the challenge presented by the North's 132 Russian-supplied combat aircraft. This was the direct result of United States policy; following repeated pleas by South Korea's President Syngman Rhee, Major-General Claire L. Chennault, who had commanded the American Volunteer Group in China during the Second World War, had drawn up a plan for a South Korean Air Arm consisting of ninety-nine aircraft, including twenty-five Mustangs.

This, however, had been rejected by General Douglas MacArthur, the Supreme Commander Allied Powers in the Far East, who believed that the build-up of such a force would serve only to increase the tension that already existed between North and South Korea. The outcome of this policy was that when the communists did attack, they enjoyed overwhelming air superiority, which they demonstrated on the first day of the war when Yak-9 fighters strafed Kimpo and Seoul airfields. These attacks underlined an urgent plea made earlier in the day to the United States Ambassador by President Rhee, who requested the immediate delivery of ten F-51s, complete with bombs and rockets, for use by ROKAF pilots.

Shortly before midnight on 25 June the US Ambassador ordered the evacuation of all American women and children from Seoul and Inchon, and early the next day General MacArthur ordered General Earle E. Partridge, commanding the US Fifth Air Force, to provide fighter cover over Inchon during the embarkation and subsequent withdrawal. The fighters were not to venture over the Korean mainland, and were to engage in combat only if the freighters were directly threatened.

The only aircraft really suitable for carrying out this patrol task, because of the distances involved, was the F-82 Twin Mustang. Colonel Jack Price's 68th Fighter

This F-82G of the 68th Fighter All-Weather Squadron fell victim to a strafing attack by North Korean fighters.

A Republic of Korea Air Force F-51D warming up on an airstrip near Kongnung.

All-Weather Squadron at Itazuke, in Japan, had twelve serviceable F-82s, but these were too few to carry out effective standing patrols. The only other unit based on Honshu that might have been able to help was No 77 Squadron, Royal Australian Air Force, which operated F-51s out of Iwakuni Air Base, but the reaction of the British Commonwealth to recent events in Korea was not yet known, and although No 77 Squadron was technically at the disposal of General MacArthur the idea of asking for Australian assistance at this stage was rejected. In an effort to solve the problem, General Partridge ordered the 339th All-Weather Squadron to transfer its F-82s from Yokota to Itazuke, and also requested the Twentieth Air Force to despatch eight F-82s

of the 4th Squadron to Itazuke from their base on Okinawa.

The evacuation began at first light on 26 June, the F-82s patrolling in flights of four just under the cloud base. There was no incident until 1330 hours, when a North Korean LA-7 fighter suddenly dropped out of the clouds and dived through the middle of an F-82 flight, firing without doing any damage and then climbing back into cloud cover. The F-82s continued their patrols during the remainder of the day, and after dark accompanied the Norwegian merchantman on which the refugees had embarked until it was met by a US destroyer escort in the Yellow sea.

The airlift of civilians from Seoul and Kimpo got under way on the morning of

27 June under air cover provided by the Twin Mustangs and also F-80 Shooting Stars of the 8th Fighter-Bomber Wing. The patrolling fighters encountered no opposition until mid-day, when five Yak-7s dived on Kimpo airfield. They were intercepted by five F-82s of the 68th and 339th Squadrons, and in a fight lasting less than five minutes three of the enemy were shot down. In the first few seconds of the battle a well-aimed burst of fire brought Lt William G. Hudson of the 68th Squadron the distinction of destroying the first communist aircraft over Korea. The other American pilots who scored were Major James W. Little and Lt Charles B. Moran. Later in the day, four Il-10 Shturmovik fighter-bombers were also destroyed by the F-80s.

With the evacuation of civilians completed, the F-82s joined other Fifth Air Force aircraft in attacks on enemy armour, artillery, military convoys, supply dumps, bridges and troop concentrations. While these attacks were in progress, four Yak-9s slipped through and strafed Suwon airfield on 28 June, destroying an unserviceable F-82 of the 68th Squadron and a B-26 light bomber. The next day, F-82s strafed and bombed enemy troop concentrations on the banks of the Han River, the 68th Squadron attacking with napalm for the first time in Korea.

The biggest American fighter effort of the day was laid on in mid-afternoon, when F-80s of the 8th Fighter-Bomber Wing, together with a flight of F-51 Mustangs which were about to be handed over to the ROKAF, orbited in relays over Suwon to cover the arrival of a C-54 carrying General MacArthur, who had decided to fly to Korea to make a first-hand assessment of the situation. An hour after his arrival, MacArthur was treated to a grandstand view of an air battle as four Yak-9s attempted to attack Suwon airfield. The enemy fighters were intercepted by the Mustang flight and not one of them escaped; two were quickly shot down by Lt Orrin R. Fox of the 8th Squadron, a third

by Lt Harry T. Sandlin of the same unit, and the fourth by Lt Richard J. Burns of the 35th Squadron.

On 30 June, General George E. Stratemeyer, Commander-in-Chief Far East Air Forces, sent a list of urgent aircraft requirements to Washington. As well as a request for an additional 164 F-80s, the list included sixty-four F-51s and twenty-five F-82s, both of which types were well suited to long-range ground attack work. The Mustangs were to be used to build up a new fighter-bomber group, to be based at Iwakuni; meanwhile General Stratemeyer ordered the Thirteenth Air Force to form an F-51 squadron at Johnson Air Base, north of Tokyo, using thirty Mustangs taken from storage. A second requirement message, dated 1 July, requested the immediate despatch to Korea of one medium bombardment wing, two F-51 Mustang wings, two F-82 all-weather squadrons, and more B-26 light bomber units. A few days later the requirement was extended to include an RF-51 tactical reconnaissance squadron.

In the event, the USAF was totally unable to meet the requirement for additional F-82s. There were only 168 of these aircraft in USAF service, and this fact – together with a critical shortage of spares – destroyed any hope of making good attrition suffered in Korea. As far as the F-51 Mustangs were concerned, the position was a little rosier; 764 of these aircraft were in service with Air National Guard units, and 794 more were in storage. Upon receipt of Stratemeyer's requirements lists 145 F-51s were recalled from the Air National Guard, and made ready for shipment to Korea aboard the aircraft carrier USS *Boxer*.

Before the deployment of these aircraft could take place, however, steps had to be taken to remedy the deplorable condition of the South Korean airfields still held by the Allies. In July 1950 the only South Korean airfield suitable for operations, even by piston-engined combat aircraft, was Taegu, known also by the military designation K-2. This was the home of the ten F-51s supplied to the Republic of Korea at the request of President Rhee, the aircraft being flown by a composite unit of ROKAF and USAF pilots under the command of Major Dan Hess (later to be made famous by the film 'Battle Hymn').

The unit was in action almost continuously during the early days of July, although its effectiveness was hampered by the fact that many of the ROKAF pilots lacked sufficient experience to handle the F-51 and also by the lack of a suitable tactical air control system.

The dangers attending this general lack of communication were tragically highlighted on 3 July, when a report that a strong North Korean convoy was pushing southwards between Osan and Suwon was received at Fifth Air Force Advanced HQ. Five Mustangs of No 77 Squadron, RAAF, now released for duty by the Australian government, were immediately detailed to take off and attack the convoy. What the Australian pilots did not know was that it was at least five hours since the original report had been sent out, and that the location they had been given was an estimated one.

Arriving over the sector indicated to them by Fifth AF Operations, the Australians sighted a long line of soft-skinned vehicles moving slowly southwards along a road near Suwon, and attacked it. Later, they learned that their target had been an ROK convoy filled with retreating troops, who had suffered severe casualties as a result of their attack. It was only No 77 Squadron's second mission over Korea, and the incident spread an air of gloom over the squadron's activities for some time. One immediate consequence was that General MacArthur ordered the ROK forces to paint large and distinctive white stars on the bonnets of their vehicles so that the latter could be readily identified from the air. No 77 Squadron's first mission had been to escort USAF B-29s attacking the North Korean airfield of Yongpu on 2 July; the squadron suffered its first casualty five days later, when Sqn Ldr G. Strout in Mustang A68-757 failed to pull out of a dive in an attack on Samchok railway station.

Although the Japan-based fighter-bombers of the Fifth Air Force were already inflicting great devastation on the North

Mustangs of No 77 Squadron, Royal Australian Air Force, prior to their departure for Korea.

Mustang of No 77 Squadron RAAF, at Yonpo, Korea.

Korean columns by the end of the second week of July - on 10 July, for example, a convoy of 150 enemy vehicles was wiped out near Pyongtaek in a massive air strike by F-80s, F82s and B-26s - the real turning point in the air-ground offensive came in mid-July, with the establishment of the Mustang-equipped 51st Fighter Squadron at Taegu. This squadron, which also absorbed the battle-weary surviving aircraft of Major Dean Hess's South Korean/American unit, flew its first ground attack mission on 15 July.

Meanwhile, USAF engineers had been extending the runway facilities of an old wartime Japanese airfield near the town of Pohang, on the east coast of Korea. Their work was completed by 14 July, and two days later the Mustangs of the 40th Fighter Squadron flew in from Ashiya. This squadron was the first Fifth Air Force unit to exchange its F-80 jets for the F-51, and

the pilots had completed their conversion to the older type in record time.

It was not long before the two squadrons, with their ability to be over the front line within minutes of a call for assistance being received, had begun to take a heavy toll of enemy troops and transport. Beginning on 17 July, the 40th Fighter Squadron, bereft of almost all communication with the outside world, undertook what amounted to a private war against a strong force of North Korean regular troops advancing down the east coast towards Pohang. Within three days the enemy force had lost all its transport, and the troops, under constant air attack by day, were forced to restrict their movements to night time. The North Korean armour suffered particularly heavy losses. The Russian T-34 tanks were found to be extremely vulnerable to napalm attacks, and both Mustang squadrons made extensive use of this weapon.

Although the air onslaught slowed down the communist advance, it could not stop it. With the United States and ROK forces being driven back relentlessly towards the Pusan perimeter, the need for close support aircraft to operate from Korean airfields was now imperative. On 23 July, the USS *Boxer* arrived at Tokyo and unloaded 145 F-51 Mustangs, pulled in from Air National Guard units all over the United States in accordance with General Stratemeyer's request. These aircraft were assembled by the Far East Air Material Command in record time and flown to Tachikawa to await collection by their pilots, who were undergoing a rapid conversion course at Johnson Air Base. The first batch of combat-ready Mustangs was delivered to the 40th and 51st Squadrons on 30 July, bringing the strength of each unit up to twenty-five aircraft, and preparations were made to move another Mustang unit - the 67th Squadron of the 18th Fighter-Bomber Group - to Taegu from Ashiya. This move was in fact delayed for a while because the Air Force engineers were still hard at work extending Taegu and the airfield was not yet ready to receive a second Mustang

squadron. In the event, the third Mustang squadron to arrive in Korea was the 39th, which exchanged its F-80s for F-51s during the first week of August and moved to Pohang on the 7th. Four days later the 8th Group's 35th and 36th Squadrons also converted to Mustangs, although both units continued to operate from Japanese bases.

By 11 August, six Fifth Air Force fighter-bomber squadrons had converted to Mustangs. These six squadrons were to bear the brunt of the close air support operations during the critical days to come, when both sides fought it out in the greatest test so far. The prize was Pusan, and with it the whole of Korea.

The Mustangs of the 35th Fighter-Interceptor Group (39th and 40th Squadrons), based on Pohang airfield, struck hard at the advancing North Korean 12th Division, but on 12 August the North Koreans entered the port of Pohang and later in the day the 35th's ground crews found themselves engaged in a series of skirmishes with communist guerrillas on the perimeter of the airfield itself. The Americans had no choice but to destroy all

RoKAF Mustang.

RoKAF Mustang.

the equipment they did not need and fly out their Mustangs to Japan.

On 18 August the North Koreans mounted a big push towards Taegu. The initial Mustang strikes during this critical period were made from Japan, the fighter-bombers carrying maximum fuel and weapons load. The Mustangs then landed at Taegu, where they were refuelled and rearmed for a new series of strikes. The Mustang pilots, ready to drop from exhaustion and suffering from extreme heat in the cockpits, operated virtually non-stop for forty-eight hours, taking a fearful toll of the enemy.

The air attacks bought time, and enabled the Americans to shift reinforcements to the aid of the hard-pressed ROK divisions. The North Koreans were pushed steadily back, and by 21 August the Allies had recaptured most of the ground they had lost during the enemy onslaught. As the Allied troops moved forward once more they found fearful evidence of the effectiveness of air support; in one place ROK troops found a stretch of road choked with the bodies of 700 enemy dead after Mustangs had made a concentrated attack with rockets, napalm and machine guns.

The main communist offensive against the Pusan perimeter began on the night of 31 August, the enemy coming on in human waves regardless of the appalling casualties they suffered. On 1 September, the Fifth Air Force's fighter-bombers flew 160 ground-attack sorties. The Mustangs proved particularly effective; on more than one occasion they enabled pockets of American infantry encircled by the North Koreans to break out of the trap by dropping clusters of napalm on the enemy concentrations.

By 7 September the North Koreans were being held all along the line. The real turning point came on the 11th when the Fifth Air Force, US Marines and SAC B-29s flew no fewer than 683 sorties against the enemy. The next day, the US Eighth Army launched a general counter-offensive and the enemy began to fall back.

On 15 September, US Marines went ashore in a big amphibious operation at Inchon, deep behind enemy lines on the west coast of Korea, and this move, coupled with the breakout of Allied forces from the Pusan sector, resulted in the collapse of the North Korean army in the days that followed. By 25 September HQ

Fifth Air Force in Korea had been re-established, while engineers reinforced the runways at Taegu airstrip to receive jet aircraft. Meanwhile, Air Force engineers had been hard at work on improving K-3 airstrip at Pohang, and by 12 October this base was the home of three Mustang squadrons - the 39th and 40th Squadrons of the 35th Fighter-Interceptor Group, and No 77 Squadron RAAF. The Mustangs of the 18th Fighter-Bomber Group were based farther south on K-9, Pusan East airfield. Meanwhile on 7 October, the F-51s of the 8th Fighter-Bomber Group's 35th Squadron had flown in to the patched-up airstrip at Suwon, but only half the runway was still usable and operating heavily-laden Mustangs from it was a dangerous business. Eventually, at the end of the month, the 35th Squadron was sent to Kimpo, where it was joined a few days later by the 36th Squadron. By this time the 51st Fighter-Interceptor Group had also established itself at Kimpo with three squadrons, the 16th and 25th Fighter-Interceptor and the 80th Fighter-Bomber, all operating F-80C Shooting Stars.

The Eighth Army now began a headlong drive towards the North Korean capital, Pyongyang, supported all the way by the Fifth Air Force's fighter-bombers, but by now there were ominous signs that the People's Republic of China was preparing to intervene in Korea on a massive scale. On the morning of 1 November a B-26 of the 730th Bombardment Squadron was attacked near Sinuiju by three Yak-9 fighters bearing Chinese Communist markings. One of the Yaks was shot down by the B-26's gunners and the others broke off when two Mustangs of the 18th Group appeared.

That afternoon, four 18th Group Mustangs were patrolling south of the Yalu River - which marked the frontier between China and North Korea - when they were attacked by six swept-wing jet aircraft. The jets made one firing pass without causing any damage, then flew back across the river. They were Mig-15s.

The MiGs appeared again on 7 November, a particularly hectic day when Mustangs were intercepted on five separate occasions in the vicinity of the Yalu. The Mustangs were hopelessly outclassed by the Russian fighters, and the American pilots had no chance of survival when attacked by a MiG except to turn inside

This 67th FBS F-51 was hit by flak over Korea, but made an emergency landing at Chinhae.

Lt David Gray belly-lands his 67th FBS F-51D after being hit by flak. The pilot was unhurt.

their adversaries, dive to ground level at the earliest opportunity and head for home as fast as possible. They were helped by the fact that the communist pilots rarely pressed home their attacks, seldom making more than two firing passes before breaking off.

During December 1950, with Chinese forces on the offensive and the United Nations ground troops largely out of contact with the enemy, FEAF aircraft were estimated to have killed or wounded enemy personnel equivalent in number to the aggregate strength of five Chinese divisions. There was evidence to show that the Chinese troops, who had initially ignored air attack, were rapidly coming to respect air power. On 28 December, for example, four Mustangs of the 67th Fighter-Bomber Squadron bombed and strafed enemy positions only eighty yards beyond Allied lines near the Hwachon reservoir, and when the attack was over more than 100 Chinese soldiers surrendered, saying that they had suffered enough from air strikes.

Faced with the Chinese onslaught, the Mustang squadrons were forced to evacuate their newly-won airfields and fly to bases farther to the south, but despite this upheaval very little operational flying

time was lost. Bad weather severely curtailed operations during the weeks that followed, but in the infrequent breaks the Mustangs joined other FEAF aircraft and US Navy Corsairs in strikes on enemy troop concentrations.

The Mustangs saw some hectic fighting in the early months of 1951. At the end of April, photo-reconnaissance revealed that the communists were building up their air defences around Sinuiju airfield, south of the Yalu, and were amassing combat aircraft there. An air strike was accordingly arranged on 9 May, and while Sabres and Thunderjets flew top cover and Shooting Stars suppressed flak, Mustangs of the 18th Fighter-Bomber Wing and Corsairs of the 1st Marine Air Wing launched bombs, rockets and napalm against pre-briefed targets in the ten-square-mile airfield area. The air attack knocked out all the communist aircraft on the airfield, set a big aviation fuel dump on fire, blew up twenty-six other ammunition and supply dumps and destroyed 106 buildings. Only one F-84 Thunderjet was damaged in the entire operation, and it returned safely home.

Airborne encounters between Mustangs and enemy aircraft did not now occur very often, but on the morning of 20 June a flight of 18th Wing Mustangs sweeping the roads south of Sinuiju ran into a formation of eight Il-10 Shturmoviks heading for Sinmi-do, intent on strafing Allied ground troops. The Mustang pilots pulled up and attacked the Ilyushins, destroying two and damaging three more. Both sides called for reinforcements, and another flight of Mustangs, patrolling over Sinmi-do, engaged six Yak-9 fighters, one of which was shot down by Lt J.B. Harrison. One Mustang was lost in this encounter. During the last week in June, on two separate occasions, six MiG-15s attacked flights of Mustangs near Sinanju and Songchon, but on each occasion the Mustang pilots outmanoeuvred the faster jets and escaped at treetop height. On 8 July, twenty MiGs attacked a squadron of F-51s returning from an airfield strike at Kangdong; the Mustangs would certainly have suffered severely had it not been for the timely intervention of thirty-five F-86 Sabres,

which shot down three of the enemy and drove the others away.

During the first half of 1951 the Mustangs, particularly those of the 18th Fighter-Bomber Wing, brought armed tactical reconnaissance to a fine art. Flying over the same terrain day after day, pairs of Mustang pilots were soon able to pick out small changes and detect more and more camouflaged enemy equipment. In February 1951 alone, the 18th Wing destroyed 728 enemy vehicles and damaged 137.

Commanded by Colonel Turner C. Rogers, the 18th Wing rapidly earned a reputation as the Fifth Air Force's 'ace truck buster' unit. The secret was thoroughness. Before a day's mission, the Wing's intelligence officers analysed the previous night's vehicle sightings and, calculating enemy vehicle movement at 15 mph, designated the areas where the enemy vehicles would have to take cover before

Recovering a damaged 18th FBG Mustang after the aircraft made an emergency landing following a flak hit near Pyongyang.

dawn. Wherever possible, Mustang squadron operations officers assigned flights the same areas or routes for armed reconnaissance each day. The first morning sortie of two Mustangs swept areas of suspected enemy activity in order to detect any vehicles damaged by night intruders and to force the enemy to camouflage, often hastily. Subsequent flights took small sectors of the assigned area or route and searched them methodically. The Mustangs flew low and slow, thoroughly searching every foot of ground, checking and double checking every building, haystack, ravine, wooded area and side road.

In the standard two-ship flight the leader flew 100 to 300 feet above the terrain, his wingman covering him from a height of about 1,000 feet. The standard truck-hunting armament load for the Mustangs was rockets and 0.50-calibre machine guns, the former being useful for suppressing flak and the latter lethal against soft-skinned vehicles. The 18th Wing pilots usually spent up to two hours in the target area. From May 1951, because of greatly increased communist anti-aircraft defences, the Mustang pilots flew at increased power settings and no longer made sorties with less than a complete flight of four aircraft.

Losses to anti-aircraft fire were high – in fact, Mustang casualties amounted to about sixty per cent of the total loss of eighty-one aircraft sustained in ground attack operations between the beginning of April and the end of June 1951 - and as a result the 18th Fighter-Bomber Group modified its tactics. Trials flown against friendly flak batteries at Seoul airfield showed that the trailing wingman in the low-level element of an armed reconnaissance flight was most prone to be hit by AA fire. In the revised tactics, the flight leader stayed low down to search for targets of opportunity; the element leader flew at 4,000 feet, searching for flak areas, while numbers two and four followed the element leader and kept a lookout for enemy aircraft. In this way, three men were covering the single pilot

who was carrying out the actual armed reconnaissance.

Considerable assistance in locating concentrations of camouflaged enemy vehicles was rendered by the RF-51 tactical reconnaissance Mustangs of the 45th Tactical Reconnaissance Squadron. On the basis of night sightings reported to the Joint Operations Centre, the 45th TRS projected the probable locations where enemy vehicles might be expected to take cover before dawn and then despatched its RF-51s on so-called 'Circle Ten' missions. These involved intensive visual reconnaissance of a circle ten miles in radius around a suspected location of enemy vehicles. After 15 April 1951, because of the growing volume of ground fire, the 45th TRS began to send out two RF-51s on these missions, one to carry out the reconnaissance and the other to watch for flak. The 45th TRS, by the summer of 1951, formed part of the 67th Tactical Reconnaissance Wing under the command of Colonel Karl L. Polifka, one of the USAF pioneers in the field of tactical reconnaissance. He was shot down and killed on operations in an RF-51 on 1 July 1951.

One of the main tasks of the 45th TRS was to maintain visual reconnaissance patrols over sectors of responsibility extending between fifteen and twenty miles forward of each army corps. Tasked with operating its RF-51s on ninety-minute flights over the enemy's front lines at altitudes of up to 4,000 feet, the squadron suffered heavy casualties, and in February 1952, after losing five aircraft to AA fire, the 45th TRS set a minimum of 6,000 feet for its visual reconnaissance missions, adding a wingman who flew 1,000 feet higher and spotted ground fire. In the autumn of 1952 the 45th TRS at last began to exchange its Mustangs for RF-80 and F-80C Shooting Stars.

Of the original Mustang fighter-bomber units operating in Korea, No 77 Squadron RAAF had now re-equipped with Gloster Meteor F.8 aircraft. The rest retained their

Air power saved the day for the Allies in Korea. An air strike goes in on a North Korean target.

F-51s, and the units involved included No 2 Squadron South African Air Force, which had arrived in Korea in October 1950 and which was attached to the 18th Fighter-Bomber Wing at Chinhae on the south coast of Korea. The first USAF Mustang unit to receive new equipment was the 40th Squadron of the 35th Fighter-Interceptor Wing, which transferred to Misawa Air Base in Japan late in May 1951 for eventual conversion to F-94 Starfires. The 35th Wing's other squadron, the 39th, was attached to the 18th Fighter-Bomber Wing for continued service in Korea in a move designed to centralize Fifth Air Force's remaining Mustang assets. The 35th Wing had rendered excellent service in Korea, culminating in a four-day period during late April when its two Mustang squadrons

mounted 400 sorties, straining its aircraft and pilots to near breaking point.

The situation was fast arising when there were not enough Mustangs to go round in Korea. General Stratemeyer made repeated attempts to replace the ageing aircraft with Republic F-84 Thunderjet fighter-bombers, but the USAF was reluctant to send increased numbers of first-line jet aircraft to Korea in view of the NATO commitment in Europe. In desperation, General Stratemeyer asked the USAF to send him some equally outmoded but more rugged F-47 Thunderbolt fighters as replacements for the Mustangs, but that request was turned down too.

The F-82 Twin Mustang was also still operational in the theatre during the summer of 1951. As a matter of routine, the

Itazuke-based 68th Fighter-Interceptor Squadron kept six F-82s on strip alert at airfields in the Seoul area during the hours of darkness and bad weather, together with some Marine Corps F4U Corsairs and F-7F Tigercats, as an insurance against surprise attack by enemy aircraft. This night-fighter defence was totally inadequate, and the USAF accordingly accelerated the conversion of FEAF's night-fighter squadrons with the Lockheed F-94B Starfire. The 68th Fighter-Interceptor Squadron began to receive its new aircraft in December 1951, and from then on maintained two F-94Bs on strip alert at Suwon.

For the 8th and 18th Fighter-Bomber Wings, No 2 Squadron SAAF and the ROKAF, which also operated a dwindling number of F-51s, there was no prospect of early conversion to more modern aircraft. In fact, it was not until 18 July 1952 that the USAF agreed to plans whereby the USAF and SAAF Mustang units would be converted to F-86F Sabres, converted as fighter-bombers, at a target date beginning in November 1952.

By the spring of 1953, therefore, apart from the handful of weary aircraft operated by the ROKAF, the story of the Mustang in Korea was over. But it had been an honourable story. For it was the Mustang which, in those grim early weeks of the war, had held the line until other combat aircraft could be thrown into the battle to gain air superiority over the enemy. Without the Mustang, the Korean War might have been lost.

Its pilots shared many deeds of gallantry. The telling of one must suffice for all.

On 5 August 1950, Major Louis J. Sebille, commanding the 67th Fighter-Bomber Squadron of the 18th Group, was leading a flight of Mustangs against enemy artillery and troops hidden along the banks of a river near Hamchang. In the initial bombing attack Major Sebille was unable to release one of his two 500 lb bombs, but despite this he circled the target and returned with the other Mustangs for a strafing attack. On this pass the Mustangs drew ground fire, and Major Sebille's aircraft was hit. Disregarding advice to head south to safety at Taegu, Major Sebille again turned into the target and fired his six 0.50-calibre machine guns at point-blank range. Somewhere on this pass Major Sebille must have sustained additional damage, for he flew headlong into the enemy concentration and lost his life. He was posthumously awarded the Congressional Medal of Honour.

Postscript

A T THE LAST count, early in 1991, 210 Mustangs were still in existence throughout the world. Some were gate guardians or on Museum display, others were in storage, and still others were under restoration – but 112 were still airworthy. Broken down, the total comprises one XP-51, three A-36s (one airworthy), four F-6s, four P-51As (two airworthy), 173 P-51Ds (ninety-six airworthy), four TF-51Ds (two airworthy), one XP-51G, five P-51Ks (two airworthy), and fifteen Australian-built Mustangs of various marks, of which nine are airworthy. These figures do not include Cavalier Mustang conversions.

It will be a long time yet before the crackle of the Packard Merlin fades from the skies.

Index

Page numbers in *italics* indicate the inclusion of illustrations, or mention in captions.